A WINE & FOOD AFFAIR

Tasting Along
the Wine Road
COOKBOOK

A COLLECTION OF RECIPES FROM
"A Wine & Food Affair"

COOKBOOK VOLUME 13

Recipes from the Wineries and Lodgings of the
Alexander, Dry Creek and Russian River Valleys.

WINE ROAD
NORTHERN SONOMA COUNTY

P.O. Box 46, Healdsburg, CA 95448

www.wineroad.com

Content © Wine Road Northern Sonoma County

Design © Pembroke Studios, www.pembrokestudios.com

Editor Linda Murphy, www.lindamurphywine.com

Illustrations © Chris Witkowski, www.chriswitkowski.com

Lodging and winery photography © Lenny Siegel, www.siegelphotographic.com

Bottle shot photography by Kelly McManus, www.kellymcmanusphotography.com

ISBN 978-1-61584-271-1

Printed in China

TABLE OF CONTENTS

TABLE OF CONTENTS

TABLE OF CONTENTS

TABLE OF CONTENTS

FOREWORD
Crista Luedtke

proprietor, boon eat + drink, boon hotel + spa, Guerneville, CA

When I think of Sonoma County, I think of the many gifts and benefits it provides – or, as I like to say, it's a boon to be here. I'm truly grateful to have moved my life to Sonoma County four years ago. There have been so many changes in such a short period of time, yet they all bring me to the same conclusion: This is where I'm supposed to be.

I began my Sonoma County experience as the owner of a boutique hotel, and now I'm also a restaurateur. After 13 years in San Francisco, I left the comfort of my home to follow my crazy dream. I remember vividly the first night at our newly purchased hotel in January 2008, we were flooded. We could have cried, but we laughed, seeing it as the Russian River's way of welcoming us with a sense of humor. From that morning on, we've dug deep, rolled up our sleeves and made this our home. I haven't looked back.

To hike among the Armstrong Woods redwoods every morning, drive along vineyard-lined Westside Road, and stand on top of Baker Ridge overlooking the Russian River Valley with friends, I think, wow…this is my backyard. I live here.

Sonoma County is a place that inspires on so many levels. It lacks pretense, has a kind of casual sensibility, and yet is incredibly sophisticated. That's the magic of this place.

I'm inspired not only by the landscape, but by what the land offers. We have the most amazing resources in this county, including world-class wines, artisan cheeses, the best meats and seafood, unbeatable fresh, local produce, natural honey and jams…and the list goes on. It's all right here.

I now have two gardens I tend with my amazing crew. We use the bounty in many of the dishes we serve at the restaurant; we don't have to look far to get the best. While some might keep such a treasure a secret, we love to share our abundance. That's what sets Sonoma County folks apart.

Many top Bay Area restaurants and chefs seek out Sonoma County products for their menus. By living here, I am fortunate to have direct access to these ingredients, and to have developed personal relationships with the people who grow and produce them. Some of the most talented chefs in the country are in Sonoma County and we have several Michelin-starred restaurants. Add to that renowned artisan farmers, affordable yet luxurious accommodations, breathtaking landscapes, and well, it really doesn't get any better.

I came to Sonoma County hoping to be a boon to the town of Guerneville and a boon to those who visited. What I didn't expect was the boon that has come back to me, in the heartfelt exchange acts of giving and receiving.

When you travel the Wine Road, remember the beauty of Sonoma County lies not only in its amazing vineyards, farms, coastal regions and redwoods, but most importantly, in its people. You may not be a local, but you are welcome to feel like one when you visit, and we hope you do so often. No matter where you are, we hope this cookbook will inspire you and remind you to enjoy life and all the gifts it brings you.

boon brussel spouts

SERVES 4 AS A SIDE DISH

Clean 1.5 pounds organic Brussels sprouts, trim the ends and cut them in half.

In a mixing bowl, combine 4 tablespoons arbequina olive oil, the juice of 1 lemon, 1/2 teaspoon each salt, pepper and crushed red pepper flakes and 2 teaspoons crushed fresh garlic.

Fry the Brussels sprouts in a commercial deep fryer (we use rice bran oil) at 350° for 1 minute and 10 seconds. Remove the sprouts from the oil and drain well. Toss them in a bowl with the above mixed ingredients and stir to coat well. Transfer the sprouts to a platter and serve them hot.

As an alternative to frying, you can also toss raw Brussels sprouts lightly with olive oil and place them on a sheet pan in a single layer. Roast them at 425°, tossing periodically, until the sprouts are crispy and slightly brown, about 15 to 20 minutes.

RECIPES

from the wineries & lodgings

BRUNCH

Pear Galette

Eggs Benedict

Bella Villa Messina Famous Hawaiian French Toast

Tarte aux Herbes

Boon Bread Pudding

Baked Eggs with Gruyère & Ham

Apple Ham Breakfast Bread Pudding

Baked Pears with Granola

Carbonara Frittata

Dawn Ranch Gravenstein Apple Pancakes

Frittata Primavera

Breakfast Bake

Crunchy Almond French Toast

Rustic Grape Tart

Bosc Pear Cake

Eggs Florentine

Hoffman House Orange & Cranberry Scones

Savory Bread Pudding with Spiced Pumpkin & Bacon

Haydon Street Inn Frittata

Sunshine Eggs

Lemon Cranberry Scones

Not-Quite-Frittata Omelette

Honor Mansion Eggs Benedict

Meyer Lemon Coffee Cake

Dungeness Crab Eggs Benedict

Polenta Crusted Quiche with Swiss Chard

Artichoke & Sun-Dried Tomato Quiche

Granny's Cinnamon Rolls

Chocolate Almond Cream Scones

Croissant French Toast with Triple Berry Cream Cheese

Andres' Ultimate Breakfast Sandwich

Healthy & Delicious Strawberry Energy Smoothie

AUBERGE ON THE VINEYARD

29955 River Road, Cloverdale, CA 95425

707-894-5956

www.sonomabedbreakfastinnwinecountry.com

At Auberge on the Vineyard, we love all things French, and our three-course breakfasts are thusly inspired. The French are very good at making fruit tarts, or galettes, as they are called. The base of this galette is a shortbread-style crust, and it's very easy to make. The heavenly aroma always draws guests out of their beds to see what's cooking in the kitchen.

PEAR GALETTE

chef Roxanne Kolbe

vegi

SERVES 6 TO 8

1 cup flour, sifted
3 tablespoons sugar
½ teaspoon salt
7 tablespoons unsalted
  butter (5 tablespoons very
  cold, 2 melted)
1 egg, slightly beaten
1 tablespoon milk
2 tablespoons apricot
  preserves
2 pears
1 teaspoon very hot water
whipped cream (optional)

In a medium-sized bowl, sift together the flour, 2 tablespoons of sugar and the salt. Cut in the cold butter with a pastry knife or fork, until the dough forms into crumbs.

In a small bowl, beat the egg and milk lightly. Pour 2 tablespoons of this over the flour/butter mixture. Stir quickly and gather into a ball. Place the ball on a floured surface and pat into a 5-inch disk. Wrap and refrigerate for at least 30 minutes.

On a lightly floured surface, roll out the chilled dough to a 9-inch round, turning it slightly each time you roll to maintain a round shape. Place the dough on a baking sheet, and fold up ¼-inch of the edge to form a rim. Brush the rim of the tart with a little of the remaining egg mixture. Brush half of the preserves over the bottom of the dough, and refrigerate until chilled.

Preheat oven to 400°. Remove the tart dough from the refrigerator. Quarter and core the pears. Slice each quarter into 5 thin slices, and arrange the slices on the dough in a spoke pattern, starting at the outside edge of the crust. For the inside pattern, reserve 6 slices, cut them in half and arrange in a circle. Brush the pear slices with the melted butter, and sprinkle with the remaining 1 tablespoon of sugar.

Cook the galette for 35 minutes and remove from the oven. Dilute the remaining apricot preserves with hot water and brush the mixture lightly over the top. Serve warm with whipped cream, if desired.

AVALON LUXURY INN

11910 Graton Road, Sebastopol, CA 95472

707-824-0880

www.avalonluxuryinn.com

The ingredients for our breakfasts are healthy and delicious, all organic, and whenever possible, are produced locally. Our organic garden, bursting with herbs, greens, edible flowers, artichokes, strawberries and tomatoes, provides us with many of the ingredients we use in our dishes.

EGGS BENEDICT

chef Hilary McCalla

SERVES 6

EGGS

1 red bell pepper

½ cup pine nuts

1-½ cups coarse bread crumbs

15 slices ham, cut into rounds

12 eggs

QUICK HOLLANDAISE SAUCE

2 egg yolks

½ tablespoon fresh lemon juice

½ teaspoon Dijon mustard

½ cup butter, melted

To prepare the eggs, julienne the bell pepper and cut the strips into confetti-size pieces. Toast the pine nuts, and set both aside.

Sprinkle ¼ cup of the bread crumbs on each of six dinner plates. Heat the ham rounds in an oven or skillet.

Poach the eggs until the whites are set – about 4 minutes. Cut the warm ham rounds into quarters, and place them on the plated bread crumbs in two circles (5 quarters per plate) with the cut points facing outward to form a star design. Gently place two poached eggs atop the ham on each plate.

To prepare the Hollandaise sauce, put the egg yolks, lemon juice and mustard in a blender. Heat the butter to very hot, without scorching. With the blender running, gradually add the hot butter. To prevent splatter, cover the blender and the vessel containing the hot butter with a tea towel while you add the butter. The sauce will thicken as it's blended; stop the blender when the sauce reaches the desired consistency.

To serve, top with the eggs with Hollandaise sauce and garnish with red bell pepper confetti and toasted pine nuts.

BELLA VILLA MESSINA

316 Burgundy Road, Healdsburg, CA 95448

707-433-6655

www.bellavillamessina.com

This is a favorite breakfast at Bella Villa Messina.
Jerry and Harold have perfected this delicious recipe over the
years and serve it on their terrace, with its spectacular views
of the Alexander, Dry Creek and Russian River valleys, with
Mount St. Helena floating in the distance.

bella villa messina famous hawaiian
FRENCH TOAST

vegi

chef Jerry Messina

SERVES 4

4 large eggs
½ cup evaporated milk
½ cup sugar
⅛ teaspoon cinnamon
½ teaspoon vanilla extract
⅛ teaspoon nutmeg
⅛ teaspoon baking soda
1 tablespoon of orange zest
  (optional)
4 ¾-inch slices Hawaiian or
  any egg bread, air-dried for
  better absorbency
corn oil for frying

In a shallow bowl good for dipping, mix all the ingredients except the bread and oil.

Coat a skillet with the oil and warm it over medium heat. Dip individual slices of bread in the egg mixture, turning over once until well-coated. Keep mixing the egg mixture during dipping, as ingredients tend to separate.

Fry the bread until browned and set, and serve with your favorite syrup and powdered sugar.

BELLE DE JOUR INN

16276 Healdsburg Avenue, Healdsburg, CA 95448

707-431-9777

www.belledejourinn.com

When I was a small girl, my French grandmother would take me to gather wild greens in the meadow near the river. We would pick dandelion, lambs quarter, purslane and rocket. This was just the beginning of the "Tarte aux Weeds." Now I tend a lovely herb garden at the inn and use its bounty in my recipes.

TARTE AUX HERBES
(fresh herb tart)

vegi

chef Brenda Hearn

SERVES 6

PASTRY

1-¼ cups all-purpose flour
⅛ teaspoon kosher salt
6 tablespoons butter
1 egg yolk mixed with 1
   tablespoon milk

FILLING

1 clove garlic
2 eggs and 2 egg yolks
⅔ cup light cream
1 cup mixed fresh herbs
   (parsley, chives, chervil,
   tarragon, sorrel), stemmed
   and finely chopped
kosher salt
fresh ground pepper

Preheat oven to 400°.

To prepare the pastry, sift the flour and salt into a bowl and rub in the butter. Mix to a dough with the egg yolk and milk. Wrap the dough in clear plastic wrap and chill for 30 minutes.

Roll the pastry to fit a 9-inch tart pan. Line the pastry with foil and bake for 10 minutes.

Remove the pastry from the oven and carefully remove the foil. Reduce the oven to 375°.

To prepare the filling, peel the garlic clove and spear it with the tines of a fork. Use the fork to beat the eggs, yolks and cream, giving the mixture just a hint of garlic flavor. Stir in the herbs and season lightly with salt and pepper. Pour the mixture into the baked pastry case and bake for 20 to 25 minutes. Serve the tart hot, warm or cold.

BOON HOTEL + SPA

14711 Armstrong Woods Road, Guerneville, CA 95446

707-869-2721

www.boonhotels.com

I began making this dish for Easter brunch years ago and it was a huge hit. The first time I tried it at boon, the guests all raved and wrote reviews, and now it's a common request. The dish has even made its way to the boon eat + drink restaurant menu in a veggie version; to make it meatless at home, substitute three cups of spinach for the ham. The bread pudding can be assembled the night before; refrigerate and bake the next morning.

boon
BREAD PUDDING

chef Crista Luedtke

SERVES 6

2 large leeks, trimmed, white parts only, cut lengthwise, then in quarter-inch slices

4 tablespoons butter

1 loaf brioche or challah bread, cut into 1-inch-thick slices

8 large organic eggs

4 cups whole organic milk

2 teaspoons salt

1-$\frac{1}{2}$ teaspoons ground black pepper

$\frac{1}{2}$ teaspoon cayenne pepper

$\frac{1}{2}$ teaspoon nutmeg

1 cup Gruyère cheese, grated

1 cup fontina cheese, grated

$\frac{1}{2}$-pound Black Forest ham, shaved very thin

5 sprigs fresh thyme (remove leaves and discard sprigs)

Preheat oven to 375°.

Rinse and drain the leek slices.

Using a 9-inch by 13-inch baking pan, take 1 tablespoon of butter and coat the pan on the sides and bottom. Place the bread slices in the pan in an overlapping shingle format.

In a frying pan, cook the leeks on medium-low heat with the remaining 3 tablespoons of butter and a pinch of salt and pepper. Cook the leeks until they sweat and become tender, about 5 to 7 minutes. Let cool.

In a large bowl, whisk the eggs, milk, salt, black pepper, cayenne and nutmeg. In a medium bowl, blend the cheeses and thyme. Sprinkle the cheese mixture and the cooled leeks over the layers of bread, then layer the shaved ham (or spinach) over the cheese and leeks. Pour the egg mixture over the ham and let stand for 20 minutes, pressing down with a spatula to submerge all the bread pieces.

Cover the bread pudding with foil and bake for approximately 40 minutes. Remove the foil and continue to bake for 15 to 20 minutes, until the pudding has an even brown color. Allow to cool for 10 minutes, and serve – perhaps with an arugula salad with fresh strawberries, toasted almonds and lemon tarragon vinaigrette.

CALDERWOOD INN

25 West Grant Street, Healdsburg, CA 95448

800-600-5444

www.calderwoodinn.com

For a touch of elegance, I usually serve our guests these creamy baked eggs in individual ramekins. Yet the recipe easily adapts to a one-dish-serves-all preparation, and the directions are included here, too.

BAKED EGGS
with gruyère & ham

chef Margaret Morris

SERVES 6

1 tablespoon butter
6 thin slices cooked ham
12 large eggs
salt, to taste
freshly ground black pepper,
  to taste
cayenne pepper, to taste
1/4 cup light cream
4-1/2 ounces Gruyère cheese,
  shredded (about 1-1/4 cups)

Preheat oven to 325°.

Butter 6 individual oval ramekins and put a slice of ham in the bottom of each. In each ramekin, break two eggs over the ham. Sprinkle the eggs with salt, pepper and cayenne pepper. Spoon 2 teaspoons of cream over the eggs in each dish and sprinkle with 3 tablespoons of Gruyère.

Bake for approximately 15 minutes, until the eggs are set around edges and lightly puffed. Remove them from the oven and let stand 5 minutes, during which time the eggs will complete cooking. Put each ramekin on a plate lined with a napkin to prevent it from sliding, and serve.

To prepare the eggs in one dish: Butter a 9-inch by 13-inch baking pan. Cut the ham into 1-inch pieces and scatter them in the dish. Break all 12 eggs over the ham and sprinkle with salt, black pepper and cayenne. Drizzle with the cream and sprinkle on the cheese. Bake for approximately 20 minutes, until the eggs are set around the edges yet still runny in the center when the dish is gently shaken. Let stand 5 minutes to complete cooking. Cut into squares and serve.

CAMELLIA INN

211 North Street, Healdsburg, CA 95448

707-433-8182

www.camelliainn.com

At the inn, we often have leftover Costeaux Bakery country French sourdough bread. I happened upon this recipe from an inn in Rhode Island and tweaked it to fit our inn's style and put that delicious extra bread to great use. Because you can prepare this ahead, you'll be free to enjoy your company in the morning. The sweet and savory taste of this dish will delight your guests as much as it does ours.

apple ham
BREAKFAST BREAD PUDDING

chef Lucy Lewand

SERVES 12

BREAD PUDDING

1 loaf day-old French bread,
  crusts removed and cut into
  ½-inch cubes
1 large apple, chopped
1 cup ham, diced
2 cups milk
7 eggs
1 teaspoon salt
½ cup sugar

SAUCE

½ cup butter, melted
½ cup sugar
2 tablespoons maple syrup

Preheat oven to 350°.

Spread the bread cubes on the bottom of a 9-inch by 12-inch greased casserole dish. Sprinkle the apples and ham over the top of the bread. Mix together the milk, eggs, salt and sugar, and pour over the bread. This can be covered and refrigerated overnight. Bake 45 to 60 minutes until golden brown. For a more custard-like texture, place the dish in a pan of water during baking.

To prepare the sauce, in a small bowl, whisk together the melted butter and sugar until the sugar is dissolved, and add the maple syrup.

To serve, cut the bread pudding into the desired number of servings. Pour the sauce over the warm pudding, so that it melts into the nooks and crannies.

CASE RANCH INN

7446 Poplar Drive, Forestville, CA 95436

877-887-8711

www.caseranchinn.com

We have served this dish eight of the nine years we have been in business. Our guests love the flavor combinations, and it seems to work well with any variety of pear that is in season. This recipe also works well with crispy apple varieties.

BAKED PEARS
with granola

chef Diana Van Ry

vegi

SERVES

4 ripe d'Anjou pears, or any
   others in season
½ cup granola
¼ cup orange juice
2 tablespoons butter, melted
ground cinnamon
ground nutmeg
ground cloves
1 6-ounce container vanilla
   yogurt
mint sprigs, for garnish

Slice the pears in half, removing the cores and stems. Evenly spread the granola in the bottom of a glass baking dish. Place the pears cut side down on top of the granola. Pour the orange juice over the pears and evenly distribute the melted butter over each pear. Sprinkle lightly with cinnamon and nutmeg, and then add a pinch of cloves to each pear.

Bake for approximately 30 minutes, or until the pears are tender (the baking time will vary depending on the ripeness of the pears). Pierce each one gently with a fork to test for firmness.

To serve, place each pear in a small bowl and top with a teaspoon of yogurt and a sprig of mint.

CREEKSIDE INN & RESORT

16180 Neeley Road, Guerneville, CA 95446

800-776-6586

www.creeksideinn.com

We serve this frittata accompanied by tomatoes from our garden.
The recipe is our most-requested one, and our guests say
the frittata, when served at room temperature, makes a great
nibble to accompany wine. It can be prepared in advance and
does not lose quality when warmed gently.

CARBONARA FRITTATA

chef Mark Crescione

SERVES 6

¼ pound pancetta, chopped
3 tablespoons extra virgin
  olive oil
½ onion, chopped
½ pound cooked ham, cubed
3 to 4 garlic cloves, chopped
½ to 1 teaspoon crushed red
  pepper flakes
1 8-ounce package dried
  linguine
½ cup grated Parmesan
freshly ground black pepper
salt
4 large eggs
½ cup cream
2 cups ricotta cheese
handful of Italian flat-leaf
  parsley, chopped
1 cup shredded provolone or
  mozzarella cheese

Preheat oven to 425°.

Heat water for the pasta in a large pot and salt it; if desired, add some red pepper flakes and black pepper to the water.

While the water is heating, cook the pancetta in a 10-inch frying pan with an oven-proof handle, until the meat is crisp. Drain the pancetta and set it aside. Add the olive oil to the pan and sweat the onion over medium heat. Add the ham and garlic. Season to taste with black pepper and red pepper flakes, and remove the pan from the heat.

When the water is boiling, add the linguine to the pot and cook until it's done. Drain the pasta, add it to a large bowl, and toss it with most of the parmesan (reserve some for layering). Season the pasta with salt and pepper, if necessary. Beat the eggs and cream together, and add the mixture to the pasta, mixing well.

Place a layer of the pasta/egg mixture in the 10-inch frying pan used to cook the pancetta, ham and onion. Add a layer of the ham/onion mixture, the pancetta and a sprinkling of Parmesan. Add another layer of pasta, then another of ham, pancetta and parmesan, until complete. Cook the frittata on the stovetop until the egg mixture begins to set, about 1 minute. Place the pan in the oven and cook 5 to 6 minutes, or until set.

In a bowl, mix together the ricotta and parsley. Remove the pan from the oven and smooth the ricotta over the top of the frittata. Scatter the shredded provolone or mozzarella over the top and return the pan to the oven for 8 more minutes. The dish is done when the cheese is melted and the frittata is golden on the edges. Allow it to cool for a few minutes, then cut into wedges and serve.

DAWN RANCH LODGE
Agriculture Bar & Restaurant
16467 River Road, (Highway 116) Guerneville, CA 95446

707-869-0656

www.dawnranch.com

Luther Burbank said, "It has often been said that if the Gravenstein could be had throughout the year, no other apple need be grown." The Gravenstein apple is so full of flavor that it's a joy to use in recipes. We are so fortunate to have this exceptional variety growing on the ranch, as the Russian River Valley is one of the few areas in the world where this uncommon tree thrives.

dawn ranch gravenstein
APPLE PANCAKES

chef Arturo Guzman

vegi

SERVES 8

1 cup all-purpose flour

1 cup cornmeal

1 teaspoon baking powder

2 teaspoons salt

2 cups buttermilk

2 farm-fresh organic egg yolks

2 tablespoons butter, melted

2 farm-fresh organic egg whites

1 teaspoon lemon juice

2 cups Gravenstein apples, chopped and sautéed in butter

In a large bowl, combine the flour, cornmeal, baking powder and salt. In another bowl, combine the buttermilk, egg yolks and butter. Just before you are ready to cook the pancakes, add the liquid ingredients to the dry ingredients all at once, stirring just long enough to blend.

In a clean bowl, add the egg whites and lemon juice, and whip the mixture until stiff peaks form. Fold it into the batter, then fold in the sautéed apples.

Heat a lightly oiled griddle or heavy skillet over medium-high heat. Pour the batter on the griddle or skillet, spacing the pancakes so they don't run together. Cook until bubbles appear on the top surface of the pancakes, and the undersides are lightly browned. Turn the pancakes and cook for another 1 to 2 minutes, until they're lightly browned on the bottom. Serve with a dusting of powdered sugar.

ENGLISH TEA GARDEN INN

119 West Third Street, Cloverdale, CA 95425

800-996-8675

www.teagardeninn.com

When I was a little girl, my German grandfather used to make something he called "goulash" for breakfast on Sunday after church. He would use whatever was in the refrigerator; boiled potatoes, ham or bacon, onion, celery, etc. He would scramble up some eggs with the other ingredients, and it was always delicious. When we opened our inn, one of the first recipes I made was a version of Grandfather's dish, and everybody else loved it, too!
I've standardized the ingredients and prepare it as a more elegant dish, yet the general idea is still the same.

FRITTATA PRIMAVERA

vegi

chef Cindy Wolter

SERVES 4

2 tablespoons olive oil

1 small red potato, cubed

1 stalk celery, chopped

½ green bell pepper, chopped

2 slices onion, chopped

6 eggs

salt and pepper, to taste

4 tablespoons sour cream (optional)

dash of hot sauce

Preheat oven to 425°.

Add the olive oil to a frying pan and sauté the potato and celery over medium heat. Add the bell pepper and onion, and continue cooking until everything is light brown in color.

In a medium bowl, beat the eggs and pour them over the ingredients in the skillet. Cook the mixture on the stovetop over medium heat for 2 to 3 minutes, to brown the bottom of the frittata. Place the skillet in the oven and bake for 8 to 10 minutes, until the frittata is puffed and golden.

Cut the frittata into quarters and serve immediately, with a dollop of sour cream (optional) and hot sauce on the side.

FAIRFIELD INN & SUITES SEBASTOPOL

1101 Gravenstein Highway South, Sebastopol, CA 95472

707-829-6677

www.winecountryhi.com

We celebrated a recent graduation at the house of my brother, James Quan, and he made this dish for our family Sunday brunch. I love the versatility of the recipe; you can easily substitute the sausage with ground turkey meat or add sautéed spinach, Swiss chard or mushrooms.
The dish is easy and quick to put together, and you can really make it your own and change up the tastes.

BREAKFAST BAKE

SERVES 6

1 pound sausage, cooked and crumbled

1 cup shredded cheese (your favorite)

1 cup biscuit mix (Bisquick)

salt

5 eggs, slightly beaten

2 cups milk

Preheat oven to 350°.

In a 9-inch by 13-inch greased baking pan, sprinkle the cooked sausage and the shredded cheese.

In a bowl, combine the biscuit mix and a pinch of salt. Add the eggs and milk, and stir until you get a fairly smooth consistency. Pour the mixture over the sausage and cheese, and bake for approximately 35 minutes, until the eggs have set and the top surface is golden.

FARMHOUSE INN & RESTAURANT

7871 River Road, Forestville, CA 95436

707-887-3300

www.farmhouseinn.com

Pretty as a picture and consistently a favorite of our guests,
this dish is our most demanded recipe and adaptable to any
season with just a change of toppings. Try it with our
Maple Pecan Butter, in-season fruit and whipped cream
— although the dish is wonderful on its own.

crunchy almond
FRENCH TOAST
chef Carol Mascoli

vegi

SERVES 6

FRENCH TOAST
8 large eggs
1 cup half and half
½ cup sugar
1 tablespoon vanilla extract
½ teaspoon almond extract
2 teaspoons ground cinnamon
pinch of salt
3 cups corn flakes, lightly
  crushed
1 cup sliced almonds, lightly
  crushed
12 1-inch slices challah bread
unsalted butter

MAPLE PECAN BUTTER
½-pound unsalted butter, at
  room temperature
½-cup pecans, toasted and
  roughly chopped
¼-cup maple syrup
1 tablespoon orange zest
½ teaspoon salt

To prepare the French toast, heat a griddle over medium-low heat.

In a medium bowl, whisk together the eggs, half and half, sugar, extracts, cinnamon and salt. Pour the mixture into a shallow baking dish. In a second baking dish, combine the corn flakes and almonds.

Working in batches, place the bread slices into the egg mixture and let them soak for 1 minute. Turn over the slices and let the other side soak for 1 minute. Remove each slice, let the excess dip drain off, and place it in the dish with the flakes and nuts, pressing the bread lightly so the mixture sticks. Flip the bread over and encrust the other side.

Butter the griddle and wait for the butter to bubble. Working in batches, cook the bread slices until they're golden brown on both sides (about 3 to 4 minutes per side). Serve hot with preferred toppings.

To prepare the maple pecan butter, beat the butter with a wooden spoon, and mix in the remaining ingredients. Serve with French toast, pancakes or waffles.

FERN GROVE COTTAGES

16650 River Road, (Highway 116) Guerneville, CA 95446

888-243-2674

www.ferngrove.com

Our guests are always impressed with this tart, yet it requires very little fuss to prepare. While it's tempting to use wine grapes in the recipe, they have numerous seeds, and their removal adds a bit more "fuss" to the dish.

RUSTIC GRAPE TART

chef Margaret Kennett

vegi

SERVES 6 TO 8

3-1/2 cups seedless grapes
1/2 cup dried cranberries
3 tablespoons cornstarch
2 tablespoons sugar
1 tablespoon maple sugar
1/2 teaspoon ground
   cardamom
1/2 teaspoon ground ginger
1/4 teaspoon salt
1 refrigerated pie crust
1/4 cup walnuts, chopped
1/4 cup brown sugar
2 tablespoons butter
2 tablespoons milk

Preheat oven to 375°.

In a medium bowl, add the grapes, cranberries, cornstarch, sugar, maple sugar, spices and salt, and mix well.

Unroll the pie crust and place it on a large baking sheet. Mound the grape/cranberry mixture in the center of the pastry, leaving a 3-inch border. Lift the edges of the dough up and over the grape/cranberry, leaving the fruit exposed in the center.

In a small bowl, mix together the walnuts, brown sugar and butter. Sprinkle over the tart's exposed fruit.

Lightly brush the pastry with milk, and bake for 30 to 35 minutes, or until the pastry is golden brown and the filling is bubbly. Let stand 15 minutes before cutting and serving.

FOUNTAINGROVE INN
Equus Restaurant & Loungebar

101 Fountaingrove Parkway, Santa Rosa, CA 95403

707-578-0149

www.fountaingroveinn.com

This recipe started as an apple crumb cake chef Doug Mahoney learned years ago. As Doug fine-tuned his culinary skills, he experimented with the recipe, switching apples for pears, and eliminated the topping. The dish has become a staple in his repertoire and a favorite on the Equus menu.

bosc
PEAR CAKE

chef Doug Mahoney

vegi

SERVES 10
½ pound sugar
½ pound butter, softened
4 large eggs
½ pound all-purpose flour
½ tablespoon baking powder
½ tablespoon vanilla extract
3 medium Bosc pears

Preheat oven to 400°.

In a stand mixer or with an electric hand mixer, whip the sugar and butter until the mixture is very smooth. On low speed, add one egg at a time, until all 4 are fully incorporated.

In a mixing bowl, blend the flour and baking powder. Blend in the vanilla extract, and then add the egg mixture, and mix just until it's fully combined. Pour the mixture into a well-greased, 10-inch springform pan.

Peel, seed and slice the pears. Starting in the center, push the pear slices into the cake batter in a circular pattern, until all the pears are inserted. Smooth the top with a spatula, and bake until the top of the cake is brown and a toothpick inserted in the middle comes out clean, approximately 90 minutes.

Garnish with fresh whipped cream and a sprinkle of cinnamon, if desired.

GEORGE ALEXANDER HOUSE

423 Matheson Street, Healdsburg, CA 95448

707-433-1358

www.georgealexanderhouse.com

We serve this dish almost every weekend, because our guests rave about the recipe. It can be made early in the morning, and popped into the oven as each guest arrives at the breakfast table.

EGGS FLORENTINE

vegi

chef Holly Schatz

SERVES 1

½ teaspoon butter
1 ounce pepper jack cheese
1 cup fresh spinach, steamed
2 eggs
1 tablespoon plain yogurt
fresh-grated Parmesan
  cheese

Preheat oven to 375°.

Butter an individual ramekin. Sprinkle the pepper jack cheese on the bottom of the ramekin, creating a well in the center. Cover the cheese with the steamed spinach.

Break the 2 eggs into the center, and bake until the eggs are set, approximately 10 minutes.

To serve, top with the yogurt and a sprinkle of Parmesan cheese.

GEYSERVILLE INN

& Hoffman House Restaurant

21714 Geyserville Avenue, Geyserville, CA 95441

877-857-4343

www.geyservilleinn.com

This scone is served on weekends at the restaurant, made fresh each morning. It's great as an accompaniment to a full breakfast or as an afternoon snack. A little dab of butter or any kind of preserves will go nicely with the scone, though it's delicious all by itself.

hoffman house orange & cranberry
SCONES

vegi

chef Danny Nooris

MAKES 24 SCONES

24 ounces all-purpose flour

3 ounces granulated sugar

1 teaspoon salt

1 teaspoon baking powder

8 ounces butter, cut into ½-inch cubes

1 tablespoon orange zest

2 eggs, slightly whipped

6 ounces orange juice

8 ounces milk

6 ounces dried cranberries

1 cup heavy cream or buttermilk

Preheat oven to 450°.

In a large bowl, sift together the flour, sugar, salt and baking powder. Cut in the butter, using a paddle attachment or the pastry knife attachment on your mixer. If you prefer, cut in the butter by hand, using a pastry blender or your fingers. Continue until the mixture resembles coarse cornmeal.

In another bowl, combine the orange zest, eggs, orange juice and milk. Add this liquid mixture to the dry ingredients, then add the dried cranberries. Mix just until the ingredients are combined and a soft dough is formed. Do not over-mix.

Flour a work surface. Take a third of the dough and turn it onto the surface. Roll out the dough in a circle that is about 1/2-inch thick. Lightly dust the dough with flour if the dough sticks as you roll it. Cut the dough into 8 wedges and place them on a baking sheet. Repeat the rolling and cutting procedure with half of the remaining dough, and finish the last third.

Once all the scones are on the baking sheet, brush the tops with the heavy cream or buttermilk. As an option, you can sprinkle the tops with granulated sugar. Bake for 15 to 20 minutes, or until the tops of the scones are golden brown. Cool slightly before serving.

H2HOTEL
Spoonbar

219 Healdsburg Avenue, Healdsburg, CA 95448

707-922-5251

www.h2hotel.com

This recipe was created by pastry chef Tosha
as a way to integrate the full flavors of Spoonbar's
Mediterranean dinner menu into the breakfast served
for banquets and to guests of the hotel.

SAVORY BREAD PUDDING
with spiced pumpkin & bacon

chef Tosha Callahan

SERVES 6 TO 8

3/4 pound day-old brioche,
  cut into 1-inch cubes

8 eggs

1-1/2 cups heavy cream

2 tablespoons sherry vinegar

12 ounces firm pumpkin

3 garlic cloves, finely
  chopped

1/2 teaspoon ground cumin

1/2 teaspoon ground turmeric

1/4 teaspoon cayenne pepper

1 teaspoon paprika

1/2 teaspoon sugar

6 ounces thick-sliced smoked
  bacon

1 yellow onion, diced

1 small can crushed tomatoes

3 teaspoons tomato paste

2 tablespoons cilantro leaves,
  chopped

1 tablespoon parsley,
  chopped

1 cup Gruyère cheese, grated

Preheat oven to 350°

Place the brioche slices in a large baking dish. Whisk the eggs, cream and vinegar together in a bowl and pour the liquid over the brioche, gently lifting the bottom cubes until all are coated. Set aside.

Peel, seed and chop the pumpkin into 3/4-inch cubes, and set aside. Whisk together the garlic, cumin, turmeric, cayenne, paprika and sugar.

Fry the bacon in a large saucepan over medium heat, until the strips are tender and slightly crispy. Remove from the pan and chop into thin strips, width-wise. In the same pan with the bacon fat, cook the onions over medium-low heat, until they begin to become tender. Add the spice mixture, tomatoes, tomato paste, cilantro and half of the chopped parsley. Combine, and add salt and pepper to taste.

Add the pumpkin to the pan and simmer for 10 minutes, until the pumpkin is just becoming tender and the sauce has thickened. Remove from the heat and allow to cool slightly. Fold in the bacon.

Lightly line a 9-inch by 9-inch baking pan with olive oil. Fold the pumpkin mixture into the soaked brioche until just combined. Pour this into the prepared pan, top with the grated cheese and cover with foil. Bake 1 hour, until a knife inserted into the pudding comes out clean. Top with the remaining parsley and serve.

HAYDON STREET INN

321 Haydon Street, Healdsburg, CA 95448

707-433-5228

www.haydon.com

Haydon Street Inn owner John Harasty was the executive chef at Churchill Downs in Louisville, Kentucky — home of the Kentucky Derby — for 12 years. He's cooked for dozens of celebrities and politicians, among them Ronald Reagan, George Bush, Burt Reynolds, Goldie Hawn and Rodney Dangerfield. Today, guests at the inn are treated to John's culinary creations, including this savory frittata.

haydon street inn
FRITTATA

chef John Harasty

SERVES 6

4 potatoes, peeled and
  cubed
2 tablespoons butter
½ cup onions, diced
½ cup green peppers, diced
10 eggs, beaten
¾ cup ham, cubed
1 teaspoon tarragon
salt and pepper to taste
¾ cup shredded sharp
  cheddar cheese
½ bunch green onions, diced

Preheat oven to 350°.

Bring a large pot of salted water to a boil. Add the potatoes and cook until tender, yet still firm, for approximately 10 minutes. Drain the potatoes and set them aside to cool.

In a cast-iron skillet, heat the butter over medium heat. Add the onions and peppers and cook them slowly, stirring occasionally, until they're soft.

Stir in the eggs, drained potatoes, ham, tarragon, salt and pepper, and cook over medium heat until the eggs are firm on the bottom, about 5 minutes. Top the frittata with the shredded cheese and place the skillet in the preheated oven until the cheese is melted and the eggs are completely firm, about 10 minutes.

Let cool for 5 to 10 minutes, then sprinkle the diced green onions over the top of the frittata. Cut it into wedges and serve.

HEALDSBURG COUNTRY GARDENS

Healdsburg, CA 95448

707 431-8630

www.hcountrygardens.com

This is a perfect quick-to-fix dish that can be prepared the night before and baked the next morning. Our guests and family love to start their wine country days with Sunshine Eggs! You can put your own spin on the recipe, adding such savory ingredients as bacon, ham, sausage and mushrooms.

SUNSHINE EGGS

chef Barbara Gruber

SERVES 8

1 cup buttermilk

1 cup Bisquick

4 cups cheddar cheese,
   grated

½ cup butter, melted

6 eggs

1 pint cottage cheese

optional (choose two):

7-ounce can chopped green
   chiles

1 cup sautéed sliced
   mushrooms

1 cup diced cooked bacon or
   chopped ham

1 cup Italian sausage,
   crumbled and cooked

Preheat oven to 350°.

In a large mixing bowl, combine the first six ingredients. Add two of the optional ingredients. Pour the mixture into a 9-inch by 13-inch non-greased pan and bake for 30 minutes. Let the eggs cool slightly before serving.

If you want to prepare the dish a day ahead, cover the mixture in the pan and refrigerate it overnight. The next day, allow it to reach room temperature, and bake at the above temperature for approximately 40 minutes.

HEALDSBURG INN ON THE PLAZA
A Four Sisters Inn

112 Matheson Street, Healdsburg, CA 95448

800-431-8663

www.healdsburginn.com

Sharon Carey has been with Four Sisters Inns since 1997 and is famous for her delicious cakes, cheesecakes, scones and more. Everyone is most impressed when Sharon is in the kitchen at the Gosby House Inn in Pacific Grove, CA. Our Healdsburg Inn guests are pleased that we use her recipe for these scones.

lemon cranberry
SCONES

chef Sharon Carey

vegi

MAKES 8 SCONES

SCONES

1-1/4 cups flour

3 tablespoons sugar

1-1/2 teaspoons baking
   powder

1/4 teaspoon salt

6 tablespoons chilled
   unsalted butter, cut into
   1/2-inch cubes

1/2 cup dried cranberries or
   blueberries

1/3 cup low-fat buttermilk

1 egg

2 teaspoons vanilla

1 teaspoon lemon zest

GLAZE

2 cups powdered sugar,
   sifted

1/3 cup butter, melted

4 tablespoons lemon juice

zest of 1 lemon

Preheat oven to 400°.

To prepare the scones, in a large bowl, mix together the flour, sugar, baking powder and salt. Add the butter, rubbing the cubes with your fingers until pea-sized pieces form. Stir in the cranberries or blueberries.

In a separate bowl, whisk the buttermilk, egg, vanilla and lemon zest together. Add this to the flour mixture, stirring just until blended.

Shape the dough into a 6-inch round and place it on a greased cookie sheet. Cut the round into 8 wedges. Bake the wedges for 15 to 20 minutes, until the scones are light golden in color.

To prepare the glaze, beat the sugar and butter in a mixing bowl. Add the lemon juice and lemon zest, and combine.

Drizzle the glaze on the scones as soon as they come out of the oven, and serve.

HILTON GARDEN INN
Sonoma County Airport

417 Aviation Boulevard, Santa Rosa, CA 95403

707-545-0444

www.hiltongardeninn.com

This breakfast dish is part frittata, part omelette. Instead of mixing
all the ingredients, including the eggs, into one batter that is then
baked – that's a frittata — chef Jose T. Contreras sautés pepperoni,
zucchini and green onions in olive oil, then adds the eggs,
where they cook on the stovetop rather than in the oven.
Yet the final flip in the pan is pure frittata; omelettes are folded.

not-quite-frittata
OMELETTE

chef Jose T. Contreras

SERVES 2

5 large eggs

2 teaspoons whole milk

2 teaspoons olive oil

2 ounces pepperoni slices

3 ounces zucchini, sliced

2 tablespoons green onion,
   finely chopped

salt and pepper, to taste

4 ounces cheddar/jack
   cheese blend, shredded

baby spinach and tomato
   peel for garnish

In a small bowl, combine the eggs and milk by whisking them together. Set aside.

Add the olive oil to a 10-inch frying pan and sauté the pepperoni, zucchini, green onion, salt and pepper on medium-high heat for approximately 2 minutes. Pour in the egg mixture and cook for another 2 minutes, or until the eggs start to firm up.

Flip the omelette over and top it with the shredded cheese. Place a lid over the frying pan and allow the cheese to melt over the heat, around 2 minutes.

To serve, top the omelette with a small handful of baby spinach and a tomato peel rosette.

HONOR MANSION

891 Grove Street, Healdsburg, CA 95448

707-433-4277

www.honormansion.com

Chef Cathi created this recipe because her husband, Steve, does not like traditional, runny Eggs Benedict. We serve this breakfast every Saturday morning for our guests, with Virginia ham, chocolate chocolate chip scones and blood orange mimosas! It is, and always has been, a great hit with our guests. Start the recipe the night before you intend to serve it, as overnight refrigeration is required.

honor mansion
EGGS BENEDICT

chef Cathi Fowler

SERVES 6

EGGS

3/4 cup half and half

3/4 cup milk

4 eggs

1/4 teaspoon black pepper

1/2 tablespoon vegetable base paste (or substitute with 1 teaspoon salt)

6 slices sourdough (or other thick bread), crusts removed

6 slices ham, cut with round biscuit cutter

6 slices tomato

1/2 cup Swiss cheese, grated

1/2 cup white cheddar cheese, grated

EASY HOLLANDAISE SAUCE

3/4 cup mayonnaise

1/3 cup milk

1/4 teaspoon salt

dash white pepper

2 tablespoons lemon juice

1 teaspoon lemon rind, grated

2 egg yolks

In a blender, mix the half and half, milk, eggs, pepper and vegetable base (or salt, if using). In a 9-inch by 13-inch baking pan, arrange the bread slices in a single layer, and pour the milk/egg mixture over them.

In a small bowl, blend the two cheeses and divide into 6 Pam-sprayed, 7- or 8-ounce ramekins. Top the cheese with a slice of ham, then a slice of soaked bread (just fold the corners in so that they fit into the ramekins). Divide any remaining liquid equally between ramekins. Place ramekins on a sheet pan, cover with foil, and refrigerate overnight.

The next day, preheat the oven to 350°.

Remove the foil from the ramekins but leave them on the sheet pan. Place the pan in the oven and bake 30 to 40 minutes. Remove the pan from the oven and let the filled ramekins rest at least 10 minutes and up to 20 minutes.

While the ramekins cool, prepare the hollandaise sauce. In a small saucepan, stir together the mayonnaise, milk, salt and pepper. Stir in the lemon juice and lemon rind. Stir in the egg yolks. Cook over low heat, stirring constantly, for about 4 minutes, or until heated to almost, but NOT quite, boiling.

When the ramekins have cooled, run a knife around the inside of each ramekin to loosen the Benedict. Place another sheet pan on top of all the ramekins and flip them over. Remove the ramekins and place a Benedict on each plate. Top each with 1 slice of tomato and 2 pieces of cooked asparagus tips, then top with hollandaise sauce and serve.

HOPE-MERRILL HOUSE

21253 Geyserville Avenue, Geyserville, CA 95441

707-857-3356

www.hope-inns.com

I came across this recipe one day and thought that it would be a great way to use some of the Meyer lemons we grow at the inn. The coffee cake can be stored for up to 3 days; the lemon flavor will intensify with time.

meyer lemon
COFFEE CAKE

chef Cosette Trautman-Scheiber

vegi

SERVES 6-8

STREUSEL
1-3/4 cups all-purpose flour
3/4 cup packed light brown sugar
1 teaspoon coarse salt
6 ounces (3/4 cup) cold unsalted
  butter

CAKE
5 Meyer lemons, cut into paper-
  thin slices, ends discarded
2 cups all-purpose flour
1 teaspoon baking powder
1 teaspoon baking soda
1-1/2 teaspoons coarse salt
4 ounces (1/2 cup) unsalted
  butter, room temperature,
  plus more for pan
1 cup granulated sugar
3 tablespoons finely grated
  Meyer lemon zest (from 4 to 5
  lemons)
2 large eggs
1 teaspoon pure vanilla extract
1 cup sour cream

GLAZE
1 cup powdered sugar, sifted
2 tablespoons Meyer lemon
  juice

Preheat oven to 350°.

To prepare the streusel, in a medium bowl, mix the flour, brown sugar and salt. Using a pastry cutter or your fingers, cut the butter into the flour mixture until small to medium clumps form. Cover and refrigerate until ready to use (up to 3 days).

To prepare the cake, cook the lemon slices in a medium saucepan of simmering water for 1 minute. Drain and repeat. Arrange the slices in a single layer on a parchment-lined baking sheet.

Butter a 9-inch angel food cake pan. Sift the dry ingredients (flour through salt) together. Beat the butter, granulated sugar, and lemon zest with a mixer on medium speed in a large bowl, until the mixture is light and fluffy, about 2 minutes. With the mixer running, add the eggs, 1 at a time, then the vanilla. Reduce the mixer speed to low, and add the flour mixture in 3 additions, alternating with sour cream.

Spoon half of the batter evenly into the cake pan. Arrange half of the lemon slices in a single layer over the batter. Spread the remaining batter evenly over the top. Cover with the remaining lemon slices in a single layer. Sprinkle the chilled streusel evenly over the batter.

Bake the cake until golden brown; it's done if a knife inserted in the center comes out clean, after approximately 55 minutes of baking time. Transfer the pan to a wire rack set over a baking sheet, and let the cake cool in the pan for 15 minutes.

Run a knife around the edges of the pan and remove the outer ring. Let the cake cool on the rack for 15 minutes. Run a knife around the center of the tube. Slide 2 wide spatulas between the bottom of the cake and the pan, and lift the cake to remove it from the center tube. Let the cake cool completely on the rack.

Just before serving, prepare the glaze. Stir together the powdered sugar and lemon juice in a medium bowl. Drizzle it over the cooled cake, letting excess drip down the sides. Let the glaze set before slicing the cake, about 5 minutes.

HOTEL HEALDSBURG

Dry Creek Kitchen

25 Matheson Street, Healdsburg, CA 95448

800-889-7188

www.hotelhealdsburg.com

At Dry Creek Kitchen, I like to serve home fries with the Benedicts. I prefer heritage eggs – those laid by heritage chicken breeds, rather than those raised on conventional farms where quantity is more important than quality. Heritage eggs simply have more character and flavor. Oven-roasted tomatoes lend great acid and sweetness to the dish; they take some time to roast, but they're well worth it.

dungeness crab
EGGS BENEDICT

with oven-roasted tomatoes, toasted brioche & heritage egg hollandaise

chef Dustin Valette, Dry Creek Kitchen

SERVES 4

OVEN-ROASTED TOMATOES
6 Roma tomatoes
1 ounce extra virgin olive oil
salt and pepper

HOLLANDAISE
2 ounces champagne vinegar
¼ teaspoon whole black
    peppercorns
¼ teaspoon whole coriander
fresh thyme sprig, leaves only
8 ounces unsalted butter
12 eggs, heritage if possible
⅛ teaspoon paprika (mild)

BENEDICT
4 ounces white wine vinegar
1 teaspoon salt
brioche bread
1 pound fresh Dungeness
    crab meat
2 cups wild arugula
black Hawaiian sea salt
freshly ground black pepper

To prepare the tomatoes, preheat the oven to 350°. Cut the six tomatoes in half and toss them in a little extra virgin olive oil, salt and pepper. Place the halves on a sheet pan and roast them for 15 minutes. Remove the tomatoes from the oven and gently remove the skins, which will slide right off. Turn the oven down to 300° and roast the peeled tomatoes for 30 minutes or so more; they're done when they have shrunk to 50% their original size and the edges have turned a golden brown. Place the tomatoes on a medium-sized plate and reserve them, warm.

To prepare the hollandaise, combine the champagne vinegar, whole peppercorns, coriander and thyme in a small pot. Heat the mixture and let it reduce until there is 1 tablespoon of liquid remaining. Strain the liquid.

In a separate pot, melt the butter and hold it in a warm area. In a metal bowl, combine the yolks of 4 eggs and the vinegar reduction, and place it on a pot of boiling water. Over the water, whisk the egg yolks until they become thickened and frothy. Remove the bowl from the heat and add the melted butter very, very slowly, as you whisk vigorously. Once all the butter is added, season with salt and pepper, add the paprika, and reserve the mixture in a warm area.

To prepare the Benedicts, in a medium pot of water, add the white wine vinegar and 1 teaspoon of salt, bring to a boil, and reduce to a simmer. This is the egg-poaching liquid.

Cut the brioche into 4 large rounds; each round should be about 4 inches in diameter. Toast the brioche until golden brown.

Put the crab and roasted tomatoes on a small sheet pan, and place it in a low-heat oven to warm.

When the poaching water is at a simmer, slowly crack 1 egg at a time into the water. Cook each egg for about 1-1/2 minutes, and place on a dry towel. The egg should have a soft, runny yolk and firm white. Cook the eggs at the last second; you want to serve them within 3 minutes of cooking.

Place each toasted brioche slice on a large plate. On top of the brioche, place some warm crab, a roasted tomato and some arugula; make a well for the eggs to rest in. Place 1 poached egg in each well, sprinkle with a little black sea salt, and top with a spoonful of hollandaise.

INN AT OCCIDENTAL

3657 Church Street, Occidental, CA 95465

707-874-1047

www.innatoccidental.com

We prepare one special hot entrée every morning for our guests, based on a two-week rotating seasonal menu. Due to the numerous compliments we receive for the Polenta Crusted Quiche with Swiss Chard, it has been served every two weeks since Jerry and Tina Wolsborn purchased the inn in 2003.

polenta crusted

QUICHE

with swiss chard

chef Tina Wolsborn

vegi

SERVES 8

CRUST

¹/₂ cup polenta

1-¹/₂ cups water

¹/₄ cup Parmesan cheese

¹/₂ teaspoon kosher salt

FILLING

2 tablespoons butter

1 cup purple onion, diced

2 cups Swiss chard, chopped

1 clove garlic, minced

3 eggs, beaten

1-¹/₂ cups half and half

salt and pepper to taste

4 ounces Gouda cheese, grated

¹/₄ cup Parmesan cheese (optional)

Preheat oven to 350°.

To prepare the crust, lightly oil the bottom of a pie pan. In a small saucepan, combine the water and polenta. Bring the mixture to a boil, then reduce the heat and stir until the polenta is thickened. Add the Parmesan and salt, mix well, and pour the mixture into the pie pan, spreading it evenly over the bottom and side of the pan. Let the mixture cool until it firms up.

To prepare the filling, in a skillet, melt the butter until it foams. Sauté the onions in the butter over medium heat, until the onions are translucent. Add the Swiss chard and garlic, and cook until the chard is wilted. Set aside to cool.

In a large bowl, whisk the eggs, half and half, salt and pepper. Add the onion-chard mixture and blend well.

Spread the Gouda cheese evenly over the polenta crust. Pour the filling over the cheese. Sprinkle with 1/4 cup Parmesan cheese, if desired.

Bake for 45 minutes, or until the center of the quiche is set. Cut into wedges and serve warm.

OLD CROCKER INN

1126 Old Crocker Inn Road, Cloverdale, CA 95425

707-894-4000

www.oldcrockerinn.com

We serve this dish every Sunday morning with chicken
sausage, cottage fries and a roasted tomato half.
It's a guest favorite. The original recipe came from
Michel Degive, former owner of the inn.

artichoke & sun-dried tomato
QUICHE

chef Tony Babb

vegi

SERVES 6

1 pie crust, refrigerated or
  homemade
6 eggs
1 cup whipping cream
¼ cup half and half or milk
1 cup canned artichoke
  hearts, chopped
⅓ cup sun-dried tomatoes,
  chopped
½ cup cheddar or Gruyère
  cheese, grated
2 pinches salt
½ teaspoon pepper
1 teaspoon Italian seasoning
¼ cup Parmesan cheese

Preheat oven to 350°.

Oil a 9-inch pie pan. Position the pie crust pastry in the pan and form scallops with your fingers all around the edge. Using a fork, poke holes in the crust so that steam can escape as the crust bakes. Bake until lightly browned, about 7 minutes. If the crust has sunk into the pie pan, push it up and reform the edge.

In a bowl, whisk the eggs. Add the whipping cream, half and half (or milk) and whisk until well-blended. Add the artichokes, tomatoes, cheese and seasonings. Mix well.

Pour the mixture into the baked pie shell and sprinkle the Parmesan over the top. Cover the rim of the pan with a crust shield, if available, or a strip of foil, to prevent the crust from browning too much.

Bake the quiche for approximately 35 minutes, until the center is set. Let stand 5 to 10 minutes before cutting and serving.

RIO VILLA BEACH RESORT

20292 Highway 116, Monte Rio, CA 95462

877-746-8455

www.riovilla.com

My grandmother, Wilma Parker, was a farmer's wife in Oklahoma, where I grew up. I watched her make all kinds of dishes out of basic ingredients and with the greatest of ease. As I grew older, I started asking her to teach me how to cook and began writing the recipes down. One memorable one was her sweet dinner roll. I thought it would be the perfect base for a cinnamon roll, and adapted this recipe from my grandmother's original.

granny's
CINNAMON ROLLS

vegi

chef Ron Moore

MAKES 24 ROLLS

½ cup sugar

1-½ teaspoons salt

2 cups warm water

2 packages dry yeast

¼ cup vegetable oil

2 eggs

5 cups flour

3 tablespoons butter,
   softened

2 tablespoons brown sugar

2 tablespoons ground
   cinnamon

In a large bowl, add the sugar, salt, warm water and yeast, and stir. To the same bowl, add the oil, eggs and flour, and blend. Knead the mixture on a floured surface for approximately 3 minutes.

Place the dough in another large, greased bowl, put it in a warm spot, and let the dough rise for 1-½ hours.

Punch down the raised dough, and roll it out on a floured work surface to form a 1/2-inch-thick rectangle. Spread the softened butter over the entire surface of the dough, and top with a light layer of brown sugar and cinnamon. Roll up the dough lengthwise, cut it into 1-inch slices, and place the slices on a greased sheet pan (close but not touching.) Let the dough rise again for at least 1 hour.

Preheat the oven to 375°, and bake the rolls for 15 to 20 minutes. Serve warm.

You can make Granny's sweet dinner rolls from this recipe. After punching down the dough, roll it into balls and place them on a greased pan. Let the dough rise, and bake at 375° for 10 to 15 minutes.

VILLAGE INN & RESTAURANT

20822 River Boulevard, Monte Rio, CA 95462

707-865-2304

www.villageinn-ca.com

Shortly after I started making bread in the kitchen at the Village Inn & Restaurant, I wanted to create something that the restaurant might be able to offer its guests as part of its continental breakfasts. I had long used a recipe for lemon currant scones at home, and with a few alterations, made a batch for the restaurant. Mark Belhumeur, co-owner of the inn, loved them and suggested that I tinker with other flavors. These chocolate almond scones soon became a favorite at the Village Inn.

chocolate almond cream
SCONES

chef Dawn Bell

vegi

MAKES 16 SCONES

2 cups all-purpose flour

⅓ cup sugar

1 tablespoon baking powder

½ teaspoon salt

½ teaspoon vanilla extract

½ teaspoon almond extract

1-½ cups heavy cream, plus some for brushing

¾ cup almonds, sliced

Preheat oven to 400°.

In a stand mixer, add the flour, sugar, baking powder, salt, vanilla extract, almond extract, cream and ¼ cup of the almonds. Mix all ingredients until the dough forms a sticky ball and all dry ingredients are incorporated. You can also mix the dough by hand in a large bowl.

Place the dough on a floured surface and form it into a large ball. Cut the ball in half and form two smaller balls. Flatten the balls to about 1/2-inch thick circles.

Brush the tops with a thin layer of cream and add half of the remaining almonds to each round of dough. Using your hands, press the almonds into the dough so that they stick. Using a dough scraper or knife, cut the two balls in half, then quarters, then eighths. Place all 16 wedges on a cookie sheet covered with parchment or coated with non-stick spray.

Bake for 10 to 13 minutes, until the scones are light brown and slightly soft in the middle. Cool before removing them from the pan. Cover securely and store in the refrigerator; they will keep for about 5 days.

VINE HILL INN BED & BREAKFAST

3949 Vine Hill Road, Sebastopol, CA 95472

707-823-8832

www.vine-hill-inn.com

This recipe can be enlarged to serve as many people as you need to feed. And croissants freeze well, so be sure to make plenty for later.

croissant

FRENCH TOAST

with triple berry cream cheese

chef Kathy Deichmann

vegi

SERVES 8

2 eggs

1 cup milk

2 teaspoons nutmeg

1 tablespoon cinnamon

1 teaspoon almond extract

1 8-ounce tub Philadelphia
   Triple Berries 'n Cream
   cream cheese

8 croissants, cut in half

6-8 strawberries

spearmint leaves for garnish

In a bowl, mix the eggs, milk, nutmeg, cinnamon and almond extract. Set aside.

Spread the cream cheese on the croissant bottoms. Slice the strawberries thin and place on them on the cream cheese, and put the other half of the croissant on top.

Spray a griddle with Pam cooking spray. Dip each croissant in the prepared batter and fry until golden. Serve with a garnish of mint leaves, and offer maple syrup, fruit syrup or powdered sugar to your guests.

VINTNERS INN

4350 Barnes Road, Santa Rosa, CA 95403

707-575-7350

www.vintnersinn.com

This makes a great "to-go" sandwich for guests on
the run — simply wrap the sandwich in foil and take
it with you. The homemade mayonnaise is a big
step up in flavor from grocery store mayo.

andres' ultimate

BREAKFAST SANDWICH

chef Andres Rodriguez

SERVES 1

HOMEMADE MAYONNAISE
2 egg yolks
$^3/_4$ teaspoon salt
1 teaspoon Dijon mustard
$^1/_8$ teaspoon sugar
pinch cayenne pepper
4 to 5 teaspoons lemon juice
1-$^1/_2$ cups light olive oil
4 teaspoons hot water

CHIPOTLE AIOLI
2-$^1/_2$ cups homemade
    mayonnaise
2-$^1/_2$ tablespoons canned
    chipotle chiles

SANDWICH
2 slices whole wheat bread,
    toasted
chipotle aioli
2 farm-fresh eggs, cooked
    over hard
2 slices pepper jack cheese
3 slices ripe tomato
2 strips crisp bacon
$^1/_4$ to $^1/_2$ avocado, sliced
sea salt and fresh ground pepper

To prepare the mayonnaise, beat the egg yolks, salt, mustard, sugar, cayenne and 1 teaspoon of lemon juice in a small bowl until very thick and pale yellow. If using an electric mixer, beat at medium speed. Add $^1/_4$ cup of oil, drop by drop, beating vigorously all the while. Beat in 1 teaspoon each of lemon juice and hot water. Add another $^1/_4$ cup of oil, a few drops at a time, beating vigorously. Beat in another teaspoon each of lemon juice and water. Add 1/2 cup of oil in a very fine, steady stream, beating constantly, and mix in the remaining lemon juice and water. Slowly beat in the remaining oil. If you like, thin the mayonnaise with a little additional hot water. Cover and refrigerate until needed; do not keep longer than 1 week.

To prepare the chipotle aioli, puree the chipotle chiles in a blender and mix in a small bowl with the homemade mayonnaise.

To assemble the sandwich, spread approximately 1 tablespoon of chipotle aioli on each slice of toasted bread. Put 1 slice of pepper jack cheese on top of the aioli, and top with the eggs, tomatoes, bacon and avocado. Season with sea salt and fresh ground pepper.

WEST SONOMA INN & SPA

14100 Brookside Lane, Guerneville, CA 95446

707-869-2470

www.westsonomainn.com

After having my son, Jadin, I was inspired by a recipe in the South Beach Diet Cook Book. I was looking for a simple way to make a tasty, filling breakfast – something that might help me lose the extra baby pounds, too. Six years later, I still make this smoothie about three times a week. Even better, my 7-year-old never turns it down. It's easy to make and very flexible; substituting and adding are no problem – ripe bananas, blueberries, blackberries and raspberries can all be tossed in.

healthy & delicious strawberry
ENERGY SMOOTHIE

chef Karen O'Brien

vegi

MAKES 4 8-OUNCE SERVINGS

1 pound fresh organic
  strawberries

1-1/2 cups fat-free or low-fat
  organic vanilla yogurt

1/4 cup raw organic almonds

1 tablespoon organic flax
  seed oil (optional)

1 cup organic fat-free or low-
  fat milk

4 to 5 Medjool dates, pitted

3 to 5 ice cubes (optional)

Wash the berries and place them in a blender. Add the rest of the ingredients and blend until all the components are integrated, approximately 45 to 60 seconds. Pour into a glass and enjoy.

Once washed, organic strawberries can go into the blender, green leaves and all. The leaves are nutritious, and there is no difference in taste of the smoothie.

APPETIZERS

Tri-Tip Cicchetti with Cabernet Reduction

Crostini con Salsiccia

Burnt Bologna Sliders

Dave's Dad's New Year's Day Clam Dip

Mushroom Strata

Zinfandel Braised Pork Shoulder on Ciabatta Toasts

Savory Mushroom, Pancetta & Thyme Tart

Peperonata - Peppers and Zucchini in Tomato Sauce

Thyme-Braised Duck with Pancetta & Porcini Mushrooms

Red Braised Kurobuta Pork Belly

Pulled Pork, Alexander Valley Style

Warm Brie Crostini with Wild Mushrooms

Grilled Lamb Skewers with Mixed Herb Pesto

Andouillette Heritage Pork Sausage with Fennel-Orange Marmalade

Saganaki

Pollen & Pork Sausage

Parmesan Roulade with Kalamata Olive & Preserved Lemon Tapenade

Cremini Mushroom Royale with Spice-Seared Pork Tenderloin

Mesquite Grilled Zinfandel Marinated Pork Brochettes

Sicilian Lamb Meatballs with Vin Cotto

Corn, Chile & Cheese Quesadillas

AMISTA VINEYARDS

Cicchetti are small appetizers served in a traditional bacari, the Venetian version of a tapas bar. Cicchetti are served with a glass of wine and enjoyed in the company of friends – the perfect embodiment of Amista: making friends. Marinate the tri-tip the night before you want to serve it.

3320 Dry Creek Road
Healdsburg, CA 95448
707-431-9200
www.amistavineyards.com

TRI-TIP CICCHETTI
with cabernet reduction & caramelized onions

chef Shari Sarabi, Baci Café & Wine Bar

Pair with Amista Cabernet Sauvignon

SERVES 6-8

2-1/2 pounds tri-tip beef, fat cap removed
2 tablespoons salt
1/4 cup balsamic vinegar
1 small onion, diced
2 cloves garlic, diced
1/2 cup olive oil
1 tablespoon freshly ground pepper

REDUCTION

1 bottle Amista Cabernet Sauvignon
1 cup rich demi-glace
1 stick butter

ONIONS

4 large onions
1 cup olive oil
1/2 tablespoon sugar
2 tablespoons balsamic vinegar
1 rustic baguette

One night ahead, salt the tri-tip and let it stand for 15 minutes. Place the meat in a zip-lock bag and add the balsamic vinegar. After an additional 15 minutes, add the onion, garlic, olive oil and pepper to the bag and marinate the tri-tip overnight in the refrigerator.

The next day, preheat the oven to 500°. Sear the meat in the oven for 15 minutes. When seared, lower the temperature to 225°, and cook the tri-tip to an internal temperature of 125° for rare to medium rare (approximately 45 minutes).

While the meat cooks, prepare the Cabernet reduction. Pour the wine into a saucepan and cook the liquid over medium heat, until it's reduced to one-third. Add the demi-glace. Blend in the butter and season with salt and pepper to taste, and remove from the heat.

Next, caramelize the onions. Cut the 4 onions into julienne strips and sauté them in the olive oil on low heat for 20 to 30 minutes. When the onions are starting to turn color, sprinkle with the sugar and balsamic vinegar and remove from the heat.

When the tri-tip is done, remove it from the oven and let rest for 15 to 20 minutes. Slice the meat and serve it on slices of rustic baguette bread, topped with the caramelized onions and Cabernet reduction.

BELLA VINEYARDS AND WINE CAVES

This little toasted delight is a Bella family favorite. The fennel flavor pairs wonderfully with a robust Zinfandel or Syrah. This recipe will encourage you to snuggle up with a glass in cold or warm weather!

9711 West Dry Creek Road
Healdsburg, CA 95448
707-473-9171
www.bellawinery.com

CROSTINI
con salsiccia

Pair with Bella Zinfandel

SERVES 4-6

3 Italian sausages, casings removed

5 ounces stracchino cheese, such as Taleggio or Robiola, crumbled

1 tablespoon fennel seeds

4 to 6 slices country-style bread

salt

Preheat oven to 350°.

Crumble the sausages into a bowl and mix in the cheese and fennel seeds. Season with salt to taste and stir well.

Spread the mixture on the bread slices and place them on a cookie sheet. Bake for 15 minutes, until the cheese is melted.

Arrange the crostini on a platter and serve them while they're still hot.

BLUENOSE WINES

In Nova Scotia, where people are known as "Bluenoses," bologna is a big part of the weekly diet. This recipe is a balance of East and West, with the bologna from the east and the Brie from the west. Rouge et Noir Brie is an award-winning cheese made in Petaluma, and is available in most gourmet grocery stores.

428 Hudson Street
Healdsburg, CA 95448
707-473-0768
www.bluenosewines.com

burnt
BOLOGNA SLIDERS

chef Paul Brasset

Pair with Bluenose Sonoma County Zinfandel

SERVES 10

1 8-ounce wheel Rouge et
  Noir Brie
1 tablespoon olive oil
1 pound high-quality bologna,
  cut into $1/4$-inch-thick slices
1 bag small, soft French rolls
Dijon-style mustard, such as
  Grey Poupon
1 apple or pear, chilled and
  sliced thin

Let the Brie come to room temperature, and cut it into $1/4$-inch slices.

In a frying pan, heat the oil and fry the bologna until the slices are blackened on both sides. Remove them to a paper-towel-covered plate.

Warm the French rolls, then spread the bottom half of each with mustard. Top with a slice of Brie, a slice of bologna and a slice of chilled apple or pear, and serve.

BRANHAM ESTATE WINES

This, like many of life's greatest inventions, started off as a New Year's Day "hangover cure" – leftover Branham Chardonnay and Dad's famous clam dip. About 20 Ruffles into the first bowl game, we realized, "Hey, this works!" Potato chips and Chardonnay are one of the best guilty-pleasure pairings on the planet; adding this delicious dip to the mix is gilding the lily in a most delightful way.

132 Plaza Street
Healdsburg, CA 95448
707-473-0337
www.branhamwines.com

dave's dad's new year's day
CLAM DIP

chef David Ginochio

Pair with Branham Chardonnay

SERVES 6

2 8-ounce packages cream cheese, softened at room temperature

2 6.5-ounce cans minced clams; reserve liquid from 1 can

2 cloves garlic, crushed

1 tablespoon mayonnaise

¼ onion, grated

juice of 1 lemon

splash Worcestershire sauce

3 shakes Tabasco sauce

pinch salt

Place the softened cream cheese in a mixing bowl and mash it with a fork or potato masher. Add the rest of the ingredients except for the reserved clam liquid, and combine until everything is incorporated.

Add enough reserved clam liquid to achieve a smooth consistency. Taste the dip and adjust the seasoning if necessary. If it needs "something," it's usually more lemon juice.

Serve with a big bag of potato chips.

FREESTONE VINEYARDS

Mushrooms and Pinot Noir are matches made in gourmet heaven, which is why we love this strata so much. If possible, use a loaf of bread from our Freestone neighbor, Wild Flour Bakery, baked in a wood-fired oven. Prepare the strata a day in advance and refrigerate it overnight before baking.

12747 El Camino Bodega
Freestone, CA 95472
707-874-1010
www.freestonevineyards.com

MUSHROOM STRATA

chef Stephen Pavy

Pair with Freestone Vineyards Pinot Noir

SERVES 6

8 to 10 slices French or Italian bread, 1/2-inch thick

3 tablespoons unsalted butter

8 ounces fresh sausage, bulk or link

3 medium shallots, minced

8 ounces white mushrooms, wiped cleaned and sliced

salt and pepper to taste

1/2 cup dry white wine such as Freestone Fogdog Chardonnay

2 tablespoons Italian parsley, minced

6 large eggs

1-3/4 cups half and half

3 ounces Monterey Jack cheese, coarsely grated

3 ounces fontina cheese, coarsely grated

Unless the bread is very, very dry, it should be toasted on a baking sheet in a 225° oven for 20 minutes a side, until the slices are dry and crisp.

Preheat oven to 325°.

Use some of the butter to coat an 8-inch-square glass baking dish. Melt the remaining butter in a non-stick skillet over medium heat. Add the sausage (if using links, remove the casing) and break it apart with a wooden spoon. Cook the sausage until it loses its raw color and begins to brown.

Add the shallots and cook, stirring, until they're softened and translucent. Add the mushrooms and cook until they no longer release liquid, about 6 minutes. Season with salt and pepper, and add the wine.

Cook the mixture briefly, until the liquid has reduced by one-half. Remove the skillet from the heat and stir in the parsley.

Break the eggs into a bowl and whisk until they're combined. Add the half and half and continue whisking. Add 1 teaspoon of salt and pepper.

Place half of the bread slices in the bottom of the buttered baking dish, tearing the pieces to compose a level layer. Spoon half of the sausage/mushroom mixture over the bread. Add one-third of the grated cheeses. Add the remaining bread slices as the next layer, followed by the remaining sausage/mushroom mixture, then the second third of the cheeses. Refrigerate the remaining grated cheese for the next day.

Pour the egg/milk mixture over all, cover the casserole with plastic wrap, and weigh down the wrap with dried beans or pastry crust stones. Refrigerate overnight.

Remove the strata from the refrigerator 1-1/2 to 2 hours before serving. Remove the plastic wrap and add the final cheese layer. Place the casserole in the oven and bake for 45 to 55 minutes, until the center is puffed and the edges have pulled away slightly from the sides of the dish. Cut the strata into squares and serve warm.

FRITZ UNDERGROUND WINERY

Jean Anthelme Brillat-Savarin said, "A meal without wine is like a day without sunshine." We couldn't agree more – particularly when that meal includes Zinfandel braised pork shoulder and a glass of wine to go with it.

24691 Dutcher Creek Road
Cloverdale, CA 95425
707-894-3389
www.fritzwinery.com

zinfandel braised
PORK SHOULDER
on ciabatta toasts

chef Ken Rochioli, K R Catering

Pair with Fritz Estate Zinfandel

MAKES 12-16 APPETIZERS

1-½ pounds boneless pork shoulder

salt and pepper

4 tablespoons extra virgin olive oil, divided

4 large shallots, halved and cut into 1/4-inch-thick slices

4 large garlic cloves, halved

1 cup seedless black grapes

1 cup apple, chopped

2 tablespoons sugar

¼ cup balsamic vinegar

½ cup Fritz Estate Zinfandel

1 cup low-sodium chicken broth

2 large sage sprigs

4 large thyme sprigs

2 large rosemary sprigs

2 large onions

2 tablespoons olive oil

1 loaf ciabatta bread

Preheat oven to 325°.

Sprinkle the pork with salt and pepper. Heat 2 tablespoons of oil in a large, ovenproof pot over medium-high. Add the pork and cook until the meat is browned on all sides, about 15 minutes. Transfer the pork to a plate and discard the fat in the pot.

Heat 2 tablespoons of oil in the same pot over medium heat. Add the shallots, garlic, apple and grapes, and sauté until the shallots are golden, stirring occasionally, about 3 minutes. Add the sugar and sauté for 30 seconds. Add the vinegar, bring the pot to a boil, and cook until the mixture is slightly reduced, about 3 minutes.

Add the wine, broth, herb sprigs and pork, with plate juices, to the pot, and bring the ingredients to a boil. Cover the pot and place it in the oven. Braise the pork for 1 hour. Using tongs, turn the meat over and continue braising until the pork is tender and falling apart, approximately 1 hour more.

While the pork is braising, slice the onions into thin crescents. In a sauté pan, heat 2 tablespoons of olive oil and add the onions. Cook on low heat until the onions are light brown.

Cut the ciabatta loaf in half and cut thin slices. Brush the slices with olive oil, season with salt and pepper, and lightly toast them in the oven.

Using a slotted spoon and tongs, transfer the braised pork to a platter. Shred the meat and tent the platter with foil. Remove the herb sprigs from the pot and skim the fat from the surface of the cooking liquid. Boil the liquid over high heat until it thickens, about 7 minutes. Strain the sauce and return it, and the meat, to the pot. Mix well. Season with salt and pepper, if necessary.

To serve, place a scoop of the braised pork on each toast and top with the onions.

HANNA WINERY

Chanterelles grow wild on tasting room staffer Patrick's property. It's a happy day when he shows up with a bag full, and they inspired this savory tart recipe. It's a perfect dish for entertaining, as you can make the tart ahead of time and serve it at room temperature. You can use any other wild mushrooms you can find. Don't be afraid of the tart dough. It's very easy to make, and tastes much better than store bought. Pancetta is unsmoked bacon from Italy, and its subtle flavor won't overwhelm the tart like bacon will. The savory pancetta, earthy mushrooms and fragrant thyme are a perfect match for our silky Hanna Russian River Pinot Noir.

9280 Highway 128
Healdsburg, CA 95448
707-431-4310
5353 Occidental Road
Santa Rosa, CA 95401
707-575-3371
www.hannawinery.com

savory mushroom, pancetta & thyme
TART

chef Chris Hanna

Pair with Hanna Russian River Valley Pinot Noir

SERVES 8-10

DOUGH
1-¼ cups flour
¼ teaspoon salt
7 tablespoons chilled butter,
  cut into chunks
3 tablespoons ice water
2 tablespoons olive oil

FILLING
1 teaspoon olive oil
¼ pound pancetta, cut into
  small dice
3 large shallots, sliced thinly
2 cloves garlic, sliced thinly
¼ cup white wine
½ pound wild mushrooms,
  such as shiitake or porcini,
  thinly sliced
½ pound cremini
  mushrooms, thinly sliced
salt and pepper to taste
1 tablespoon fresh thyme
1 cup fresh pecorino, grated
1 tablespoon fresh parsley,
  chopped

Preheat oven to 375°.

To prepare the tart dough, pulse the flour and salt in a food processor until they're blended. Add the chunks of butter and blend just until the mixture resembles pebbles. Add the ice water and pulse just until the mixture comes together. Do not let form into a ball. Turn out the dough onto a floured surface and shape it into a disk. Wrap the disk in waxed paper and let it rest at least 1 hour.

Roll out the tart to a rectangular shape. Fit the dough into a tart pan, pushing the dough up the sides. Trim the dough flush with the rim of the pan. Prick the dough all over with a fork. Bake for 20 minutes, or until the shell is light golden.

Meanwhile, prepare the filling. In a large saucepan, heat the olive oil to shimmering over medium heat. Add the pancetta to the pan and brown, allowing the fat to render. Add the shallots and sauté until they're translucent. Add the garlic and sauté for 1 minute. Add the wine, scraping up any brown bits in the pan. Add the sliced mushrooms and sauté for 5 to 10 minutes, until the mushrooms are cooked through; cover pan, if needed, to release more moisture from the mushrooms.

Add salt and pepper to taste. Add the thyme. Allow the filling to cool slightly.

Scatter the pecorino evenly over the tart shell. Fill the shell with the mushroom mixture.

Return the tart to the oven and bake for an additional 10 minutes. Allow it to cool slightly. Scatter fresh parsley over the top of the tart, cut and serve.

LAGO DI MERLO
VINEYARDS & WINERY

"Chi non lavora, non deve mangiare." Translation: "If you don't work, you don't eat." This quote hung on the wall in the boarding house operated by Clotilde Merlo. Like many good Italian chefs, Clotilde used ingredients available to her and in measurements known only to her. A handful of this, a pinch of that, and then magic! You'll find some in this peperonata, a traditional Merlo family recipe. You can substitute fresh, in-season Italian green beans for the zucchini.

4791 Dry Creek Road
Healdsburg, CA 95448
707-433-0100
www.familywines.com

PEPERONATA
(peppers & zucchini in tomato sauce)

Recipe by Clotilde Merlo

vegi

Pair with Lago di Merlo Dry Creek Valley Sangiovese

MAKES 2 CUPS

¼ cup olive oil

1-½ pounds zucchini, sliced into 1/8-inch rounds

1 red bell pepper, cored and thinly sliced

1 green pepper, cored and thinly sliced

1 yellow onion, coarsely chopped

2 cloves garlic, diced

2 stalks celery, coarsely chopped

3 medium-large tomatoes, peeled and chopped

½ cup Italian parsley, finely chopped

Heat the olive oil in a large, shallow frying pan. Add the zucchini, peppers, onion, garlic and celery. Stir on high for 5 to 10 minutes. Add the tomatoes and parsley, and stir together.

Cover the pan with a lid and cook down the mixture on medium-low heat for 20 minutes, or until the liquid is absorbed and zucchini is cooked, but still somewhat firm. If the zucchini starts to fall apart, you've overcooked it.

Let the peperonata cool and refrigerate overnight for the best flavor development. Bring it to room temperature, and serve it on rustic Italian bread and a drizzle of olive oil. It's also great with grilled fish and roast chicken.

LONGBOARD VINEYARDS

This is the perfect gourmet treat to serve your guests during the holiday season. The fireplace is crackling, it's cold outside and you've just poured your favorite Longboard wine, Dakine Syrah.

5 Fitch Street
Healdsburg, CA 95448
707-433-3473
www.longboardvineyards.com

THYME-BRAISED DUCK

with pancetta & porcini mushrooms

chef Heidi West, Heidi West Catering

Pair with Longboard Dakine Syrah

SERVES 2

2 large duck legs, 8 to 10 ounces each, trimmed of fat

½ tablespoon thyme leaves plus 2 whole sprigs

1/2 tablespoon freshly cracked black pepper

2 cloves garlic, minced

¼-ounce dried porcini mushrooms

1 cup boiling water

2 tablespoons extra virgin olive oil

1 ounce pancetta, finely diced

½ medium onion, diced

¼ cup fennel bulb, diced

¼ cup carrot, diced

1 bay leaf

1 cup Longboard Dakine Syrah

1 tablespoons balsamic vinegar

1 cup chicken stock

Preheat oven to 325°.

Season the duck with the thyme leaves, pepper and garlic. Cover and refrigerate 4 hours or overnight.

In a small bowl, soak the dried porcini in the 1 cup of boiling water, until the porcini are softened, about 20 minutes. Using your fingers, rub any grit off the mushrooms in the soaking liquid. Drain the mushrooms, reserving the soaking liquid; squeeze any excess liquid from the mushrooms and coarsely chop them. Slowly pour the soaking liquid into a cup, stopping before you reach the grit at the bottom.

Take the duck out of the refrigerator and season the legs on all sides with salt. Heat a large skillet over high heat. Add the olive oil. Place the duck legs in the skillet, skin side down. Cook until the skin is deep golden brown and crispy. Turn the legs, reduce the heat to medium, and cook for 2 minutes.

Transfer the duck to a Dutch oven, skin side up. Discard half of the fat in the skillet. Heat the skillet over medium heat. Add the pancetta and cook until it's lightly browned. Add the onion, fennel, carrot, thyme sprigs and bay leaf. Cook, stirring often to scrape up all the crusty bits, until the vegetables are browned, about 10 minutes.

Add the wine and vinegar. Turn the heat to high and bring the liquid to a boil. Cook until it has reduced by half, 6 to 8 minutes. Add the chicken stock and reserved porcini liquid, bring to another boil, and turn the heat to low. Simmer for 5 minutes. Add the broth, vegetables and chopped porcinis to the Dutch oven (the liquid should not quite cover the duck; add more stock if necessary). Cover the pan with foil and a lid, and place in the oven until the duck is very tender, about 2-½ hours.

Transfer the duck to a pan and allow it to cool. Shred the duck with your fingers. Strain the broth reserving the vegetables. Skim the top layer of fat from the sauce. Reduce the broth over medium-high heat to thicken. Add the vegetable mixture to the shredded duck and moisten with sauce reduction.

Season to taste with salt and pepper, and serve on baguette slices or crostini.

MALM CELLARS

This is, hands down, the best appetizer at the Cat & the Custard Cup restaurant in La Habra, Calif. Chef Creed Salisbury was kind enough to share this recipe with us, and it's a heavenly match with Malm Pinot Noir. Start the recipe one day in advance; wasabi paste and unagi (eel) glaze can be found in Asian markets; most grocery stores carry wasabi paste.

119 W. North Street
Healdsburg, CA 95448
707-364-0441
www.malmcellars.com

red braised

KUROBUTA PORK BELLY

with wasabi mashed potato, unagi glaze & natural jus

Recipe created by chef Creed Salisbury, the Cat & Custard Cup

Pair with Malm Sonoma Coast Pinot Noir

SERVES 10

PORK BELLY

5-pound slab Kurobuta pork belly

peanut oil

BRAISING LIQUID

1-1/3 cups soy sauce

2/3 cup sugar

8 cups water

6 cloves garlic, smashed

3 star anise pods

2 teaspoons black peppercorns

2 tablespoons chopped fresh ginger

ASSEMBLY

wasabi paste, purchased

unagi glaze, purchased

your favorite mashed potato recipe

sesame seeds, toasted

Cut the pork belly into 4 equal pieces. Heat the oil in a sauté pan over high heat, and add the pork belly, skin side down. Cook on all sides until the exterior is browned, and set the pork aside.

In a large Dutch oven, combine all braising liquid ingredients and bring to a boil. Add the browned pork belly and return the mixture to a boil. Lower the heat to simmer, cover the Dutch oven, and braise the pork belly until it's tender, approximately 2-1/2 to 3 hours.

Gently place the pork belly in a separate container. Strain the braising jus, discard the solids, and pour the liquid over the pork. Let it cool, and refrigerate overnight

The next day, remove the pork from the jus and slice it lengthwise into 1/2-inch-wide strips. Sauté both sides in peanut oil until the strips are crispy. In a small saucepan, reduce the braising jus to the desired consistency, and set aside.

Whisk the wasabi paste into your prepared mashed potatoes; the amount of wasabi paste depends on your heat preference. Spoon the potatoes onto individual plates and place the desired amount of pork belly strips on top. Ladle some reduced braising jus around the plate, lightly drizzle unagi glaze over the pork belly, and finish with a sprinkling of toasted sesame seeds. Serve warm.

MANTRA WINES

Great wine makes great barbecue, any time of year. This recipe can be prepared for a crowd, or make it for your family and enjoy the leftovers the next day. Don't forget to pair the pork with Zinfandel.

779 Westside Road
Healdsburg, CA 95448
707-433-2900
www.mantrawines.com

PULLED PORK
alexander valley style

chef Christine Cureton

Pair with Mantra Old Vines Zinfandel

MAKES 20 APPETIZER SERVINGS

ZINFANDEL SAUCE

1-1/2 cups Mantra Old Vines
   Zinfandel

1/3 cup brown sugar

1/2 teaspoon (or less) cayenne

1/2 teaspoon pepper

1 teaspoon salt

2 oregano sprigs

PORK

5 pounds pork shoulder

garlic powder

salt and pepper

20 soft slider rolls

Preheat oven to 300°.

To prepare the Zinfully Spicy BBQ sauce, add all the ingredients to a large stockpot and blend well. Simmer on medium-low heat for 1 hour. Let cool before serving. The sauce can made 1 day ahead; refrigerate overnight, and allow it to come to room temperature before serving.

Rub the pork shoulder with garlic powder, salt and pepper, and let stand for at least 1 hour.

Roast the pork for 4 to 4-1/2 hours, checking the internal temperature at 3 hours with a meat thermometer; roast until the temperate reaches 170°. Let the meat sit for 10 minutes, then pull it apart with forks.

Once all the pork is shredded, saturate it in the Zinfully Spicy BBQ Sauce, to taste. Place a generous mound of the meat/sauce mixture on the soft slider rolls, and serve.

MIETZ CELLARS

Nancy Mietz has made these crostini for special events at the winery for many years and they're always a crowd favorite. They're easy to prepare, too.

4791 Dry Creek Road
Healdsburg, CA 95448
707-433-0100
www.familywines.com

WARM BRIE CROSTINI
with wild mushrooms

vegi

chef Susan Mall, Zin Restaurant & Wine Bar

Pair with Mietz Pinot Noir

SERVES 8-12

2 tablespoons unsalted butter

6 ounces crimini mushrooms, halved or quartered

6 ounces shiitake mushrooms, stemmed, caps sliced

2 tablespoons shallots, minced

½ cup Pinot Noir

2 teaspoons fresh thyme, chopped

salt and freshly ground black pepper

1 (14 ounce) ripe Brie cheese, about 5 inches in diameter

1 baguette, cut into ¼-inch-thick slices and toasted

Melt the butter in a large skillet over medium-high heat. Add the crimini and shiitake mushrooms and cook, stirring occasionally, until the mushrooms begin to brown, about 8 minutes. Add the shallots and stir until they soften, about 1 minute.

Add the Pinot Noir, bring it to a boil, and cook until the wine is almost completely evaporated, about 5 minutes. Stir in the thyme. Season with salt and pepper. Remove the skillet from the heat and let the mixture cool.

The mushrooms can be made up to 1 day ahead, cooled, covered and refrigerated. Bring them to room temperature before proceeding.

Remove the Brie from the wrapper. Using a sharp knife, cut off and discard the top rind from the cheese. Place the cheese in an attractive baking dish, cut side up. Mound the mushrooms on top of the cheese. (The cheese can be prepared and refrigerated up to 8 hours before baking.)

Position a rack in the center of the oven and preheat to 350°. Bake the cheese until it begins to melt, about 15 minutes. Transfer the cheese in its dish to a warming tray or chafing dish, and serve hot with toasted baguette slices, allowing guests to scoop and spread the cheese and mushrooms onto the bread.

MILL CREEK WINERY

Making your own herbed pesto is well worth the effort for its fresh and complex taste. It will keep for up to a week in the refrigerator, and you can use it as a dip, on sandwiches or over pasta.

1401 Westside Road
Healdsburg, CA 95448
707-431-2121
www.millcreekwinery.com

GRILLED LAMB SKEWERS
with mixed herb pesto

chef Domenica Catelli, Catelli's restaurant

Pair with Mill Creek Zinfandel

SERVES 8

PESTO

2 tablespoons pine nuts, toasted

2 large cloves garlic

1-1/2 cups fresh flat-leaf parsley

1 cup mixed fresh herbs (mint, basil, dill, oregano or thyme)

1/4 cup Parmesan cheese, freshly grated

1/3 cup extra virgin olive oil

1/4 teaspoon salt

LAMB

1 pound lamb flank or loin

1/4 cup Mixed Herb Pesto (see recipe)

salt

fresh-cracked black pepper

bamboo skewers

To prepare the pesto, put all ingredients except the oil in a food processor. Begin to pulse. With the processor on, slowly pour the oil through the food chute. Process until the ingredients are well blended and spoon into an airtight container. Store in the refrigerator for up to 1 week.

To prepare the lamb, generously coat the loin or flank in pesto and let it marinate for 20 minutes at room temperature, then overnight in the refrigerator. The longer the marinating time, the more intense the flavor.

Sprinkle the lamb with salt and pepper and cook it over a gas or charcoal grill on high heat, until the meat is medium-rare; the cooking time will depend on the thickness of the meat.

Remove the lamb from the grill, let it rest for 10 minutes, then cut it into 1/4-inch-thick strips. Skewer the strips and finish them with a drizzle of the remaining herb pesto.

QUIVIRA VINEYARDS AND WINERY

At Quivira, we love pigs – we raise them, feature them on our wine labels, and our mascot, Ruby the wild pig, has even made the Los Angeles Times newspaper! Our love of pigs, Biodynamic farming, bees and unique wines all come together in this recipe. Look for Sonoma County local Elissa Rubin-Mahon's Artisan Preserves marmalade used in this recipe.

4900 West Dry Creek Road
Healdsburg, CA 95448
707-431-8333
www.quivirawine.com

"andouillette" gloucestershire old spot
HERITAGE PORK SAUSAGE
with fennel-orange marmalade

chef Joe Rueter, theGreenGrocer

Pair with Quivira Wine Creek Ranch Mourvedre

SERVES 4-6

2 fennel bulbs, whole with tops

1 teaspoon black pepper, ground

1 tablespoon unsalted butter

4 ounces Artisan Preserves Orange Honey Marmalade

3 tablespoons extra virgin olive oil (preferably Quivira Estate Extra Virgin Olive Oil)

2 teaspoons kosher salt

1 pound Quivira "Andouillette" Heritage Pork Sausage

Remove and reserve the green tops from the fennel. Wash and dice the white fennel bulbs.

Heat a large sauté pan with a tight-fitting lid over medium heat. Add the black pepper and toast it, dry, until it's aromatic. Add the butter and diced fennel to the pan. Cover and reduce the heat to medium-low. Cook, covered, stirring occasionally, for 5 to 6 minutes, or until the fennel is tender and translucent.

Meanwhile, place the marmalade on a clean cutting board and chop it fine with a sharp knife. Scrape the marmalade into a mixing bowl. Finely chop 1/2 of the fennel tops and mix them with the marmalade. When the fennel butter is finished cooking, stir in the olive oil and remove the pan from the heat.

Allow the fennel butter to cool slightly, then incorporate it with the marmalade-fennel top mixture. Season with salt, and spread the mixture on a sheet pan lined with parchment paper. Refrigerate to cool and set the color.

Cook the sausages on a hot grill or in a preheated heavy cast iron skillet. The intent is to give the exterior of the sausage a browning; cooking should take about 10 minutes. Allow the sausage to rest for at least 5 minutes, then slice into 1-inch-thick rounds. Reserve in a warm place.

Reheat the orange-honey-fennel marmalade and place the desired portion onto each plate. Arrange the sausage on top and garnish with a few small sprigs of the reserved fennel tops.

ROADHOUSE WINERY

We first had saganaki, a flaming Greek cheese appetizer, at "A Wine & Food Affair" and loved the way it brought out the flavors in a variety of wines. It's also wonderful to watch it being made, with the flambéed cheese becoming a delicious fondue. Our Eric's Red Blend brings out the herbs and subtle flavors of saganaki, while the dish accentuates the deep red berries and spice in the wine.

240 Center Street
Healdsburg, CA 95448
707-922-6362
www.roadhousewinery.com

SAGANAKI

chef Eric Anderson

vegi

Pair with Roadhouse Eric's Red Blend

SERVES 2

8 ounces kasseri cheese, cubed

3/4 teaspoon strong red wine vinegar

3/4 teaspoon lemon juice

1/4 teaspoon Greek oregano

1-1/2 tablespoons Metaxa (Greek brandy)

In a skillet, melt the cheese over medium heat, stirring occasionally. Whisk in the vinegar and lemon juice, raise the heat to high briefly, and sprinkle the oregano over the top.

Drizzle the cheese with the Metaxa and carefully ignite it with a long-handled barbecue lighter, quickly stepping back from the flames. They should die down in a few seconds, but have a large metal lid on hand to cover the flames, should they get out of hand.

Serve the saganaki hot, cut into wedges and plated, or simply let your guests dip pita chips or pita bread into the cheese, straight from the skillet.

ROUTE 128 VINEYARDS & WINERY

Our family gatherings would not be the same without starting with nephew and chef Rian's homemade sausages and a glass of wine; the sausage flavor of the day is always at Rian's whim. For the fortunate loyalists of Route 128 who have enjoyed Rian's sausages in the past, we coerced him to put yet another magical recipe down on paper.

21079 Geyserville Avenue, Suite 2
Geyserville, CA 95441
707-696-0004
www.route128winery.com

POLLEN & PORK SAUSAGE

chef Rian Rinn

Pair with Route 128 Syrah

MAKES 20 LINKS

5 pounds pork butt

3 tablespoons salt

1/2 cup walnuts, coarsely
  chopped

1 teaspoon allspice

1/2 tablespoon black pepper

1/4 teaspoon cayenne

zest of 1 lemon

1/2 tablespoon garlic, finely
  chopped

1/8 cup parsley, coarsely
  chopped

2 cups Route 128 Syrah

1/8 cup bee pollen

3 yards of hog casings

Grind the pork to coarse ground (or with a 1/8-inch die). In a large bowl, add all the ingredients except for the bee pollen and hog casings, and mix thoroughly. Add more wine if the mixture appears to be too dry.

Sprinkle the bee pollen evenly over the meat, and add the mixture to a sausage stuffer. Stuff the pork loosely into the casing, pricking with the tip of a sharp paring knife every few inches of filled casing. Twist the casing to tighten the links.

Let the links sit overnight in the refrigerator. To serve, grill the links over medium heat until they're browned and cooked through, and serve.

SOUVERAIN
AT ASTI WINERY

This recipe is a culinary trifecta. First, it's easy to prepare. Second, it tastes amazingly good. And third, the smell ... well, when this little jewel is baking in the oven, the aroma entices everyone to the kitchen. Prepare and freeze the pastry one day before you plan to serve the roulade.

26150 Asti Road
Cloverdale, CA 95425
707-265-5490
www.souverain.com

PARMESAN ROULADE

with kalamata olive & preserved lemon tapenade

vegi

chef Maurine Sarjeant

Pair with Souverain Russian River Valley Chardonnay

SERVES 40

PASTRY

1 sheet frozen puff pastry
dough

4 ounces clarified butter

1 head garlic, roasted and
pureed

4 ounces Parmesan cheese,
finely grated

TAPENADE

4 ounces kalamata olives,
pitted

1 ounce preserved lemon
(find in fine food stores)

1 shallot, peeled and
chopped

1 teaspoon lemon juice

To prepare the pastry, thaw the puff pastry dough sheet and roll it out to $1/8$-inch thick. Keep the shape rectangular. Brush the entire top with clarified butter, then spread with the garlic puree. Sprinkle with the Parmesan.

Turn the pastry so that the long side faces you. Roll it into a log, tightly but gently. Brush the end with clarified butter to seal the dough, wrap it in plastic wrap, and freeze.

When you're ready to prepare the appetizer, remove the roll from the freezer and let it thaw to a semi-frozen state. It's important to keep the roll partially frozen. While the roll thaws, prepare the tapenade by placing all the ingredients in a food processor, and pulsing until everything is semi-finely minced. Set aside.

Preheat oven to 425˚.

Slice the semi-frozen roll very thinly, on an angle, with a serrated knife. Place the slices on a sheet pan fitted with a silicone nonstick baking mat or parchment paper. Bake the slices for 10 to 12 minutes, until they're golden brown. Top with the tapenade and serve warm.

TRIONE VINEYARDS & WINERY

With our first month coming to a close and after an insanely busy day in January, we gathered on the veranda and opened a bottle of our Pinot Noir. Our friend, Chef Tim, brought a sample of a dish he was developing for our wine club dinner. That sunny, crisp winter evening was the perfect setting in which to enjoy the rich custard and earthy mushrooms of Tim's creation. Paired with our Pinot Noir, it's as if Ginger Rogers and Fred Astaire are dancing on your tongue.

19550 Geyserville Avenue
Geyserville, CA 95441
707-814-8100
www.trionewinery.com

CREMINI MUSHROOM ROYALE

with spice-seared pork tenderloin

chef Tim Vallery, Peloton Catering

Pair with Trione Russian River Valley Pinot Noir

MAKES 48 APPETIZERS

SPICED PORK

¼ cup olive oil

3 Berkshire boneless pork tenderloins, trimmed and cleaned

your favorite spice blend, for rubbing pork

CUSTARD

1 quart heavy cream

2 bunches thyme

1 bay leaf

1 tablespoon whole black peppercorns

1-¼ cups shallots, minced

3 tablespoons garlic, minced

2 tablespoons olive oil

1-½ pounds cremini mushrooms, roasted

1 tablespoon kosher salt

1 teaspoon black pepper, freshly ground

4 eggs (2 whole eggs plus 2 yolks), lightly whipped

1 tablespoon fresh thyme, chopped

Preheat oven to 400°.

To prepare the pork, heat a large, deep skillet over medium flame and coat with the oil. Dredge the tenderloins in the spice mix and sauté them until the meat is well caramelized. Remove the tenderloins from the pan, place them on a baking sheet and cook in the preheated oven until the meat is medium rare.

Let the cooked pork cool for 20 minutes, then place it in the refrigerator to chill while you prepare the custard. Lower the oven temperature to 325°.

To prepare the custard, in a large saucepan, bring the cream, thyme, bay leaf and peppercorns to a simmer. Let the mixture simmer for 5 minutes, and then let it rest for 30 minutes.

In another pot, sweat the shallots and garlic in the olive oil. After 2 or 3 minutes, add the mushrooms and continue to simmer until the liquid in the mushrooms has reduced. Remove the pot from the heat.

Strain the cream mixture through a fine strainer into the mushrooms. Temper the eggs into the mixture and add the thyme. Place this mixture in a well-oiled, nonstick mini-muffin pan. Place the pan in a water bath and bake the custard until it's slightly firm, about 20 minutes. Let it cool, then carefully unmold onto a plate.

To serve, thinly slice the chilled pork tenderloins. Place 3 slices of pork on each the plate and top with the custard.

TRUETT HURST WINERY

This is a wonderful fall dish, and a great way to use up the last tomatoes of the season, while also sneaking in one last barbecue before the rains come. Kick back with a glass of Truett Hurst Zinfandel, and enjoy these brochettes right off the grill.

5610 Dry Creek Road
Healdsburg, CA 95448
707-433-9545
www.truetthurst.com

mesquite grilled zinfandel-marinated
PORK BROCHETTES
glazed with tomato shallot jam

chef Peter Brown, Jimtown Store

Pair with Truett Hurst Red Rooster Zinfandel

SERVES 6-8

PORK

½ cup Truett Hurst Red Rooster
    Zinfandel

1 tablespoon Dijon mustard

2 garlic cloves, minced

1 teaspoon fresh thyme, chopped

1 teaspoon fresh oregano, chopped

1 tablespoon fresh parsley, chopped

2 teaspoons kosher salt

1 teaspoon coarsely ground black
    pepper

2 tablespoons olive oil

1 pork tenderloin (12-16 ounces), split
    lengthwise and cut into 1-inch
    pieces

1 bunch green onions, cut into 1-inch
    pieces

2 small zucchini or yellow squash,
    cut into thin rounds

12-16 skewers

TOMATO JAM

1 teaspoon black mustard seeds

2 teaspoons olive oil

½ cup shallots, sliced into thin rings

2 cups peeled, seeded tomatoes,
    medium dice

1 cup sugar

1 tablespoon tamarind paste

pinch salt

To prepare the pork, in a large mixing bowl, whisk together the wine, mustard, garlic, herbs, salt, pepper and olive oil. Add the pork pieces and mix well. Allow the pork to marinate for at least 30 minutes.

Meanwhile, prepare the jam. Heat a small, heavy skillet on medium heat and add the mustard seeds. As soon as they start to pop, add the oil and shallots. Sauté until the shallots are golden brown, then add the tomatoes, sugar, tamarind paste and salt. Cook the mixture until it reduces and becomes thick, with a jam-like consistency.

Skewer the marinated pork pieces with alternating pieces of green onion and zucchini. Grill the pork over a hot mesquite grill to an internal meat temperature of at least 145° – longer if you like your pork tenderloin well done. In the last few minutes of cooking, brush the brochettes with the jam, turning the skewers to caramelize the meat on all sides. Serve as is, or on a bed of baby spinach or arugula, if desired.

TWOMEY CELLARS

This simple hors d'oeuvre pairs beautifully with red wine and can be prepared in advance, to take to your next party. At the winery, we make our own vin cotto ("cooked wine"), in the Old World method, by slowly simmering wine lees for four to five days. This produces a rich and sweet condiment sauce with a consistency similar to that of well-aged balsamic vinegar. Vin cotto can be purchased at gourmet grocery stores; if you can't find it, use aged balsamic.

3000 Westside Road
Healdsburg, CA 95448
707-942-7120
www.twomeycellars.com

SICILIAN LAMB MEATBALLS
with vin cotto

chef Dominic Orsini

Pair with Twomey Merlot or Pinot Noir

MAKES 24 MEATBALLS

¼ cup olive oil

¼ cup shallots, minced

2 medium cloves garlic, minced

¼ teaspoon black pepper

¼ teaspoon ground coriander

2 teaspoons salt

2 large eggs

1 pound ground lamb

¼ cup unseasoned bread crumbs

¼ cup preserved lemon, small dice

¼ cup pistachios, toasted

¼ cup olives, chopped

small bottle of vin cotto or 20-year balsamic

Preheat oven to 500°.

In a small sauté pan over very low heat, add the olive oil, shallots and garlic. Stir often and let the mixture cook for 10 minutes, or until the shallots are translucent. Add the pepper, coriander and salt to the pan, stir, and cook for an additional 1 minute. Transfer the mixture to a plate to cool.

In a small bowl, scramble the eggs together and add the cooled shallots and garlic.

Place the ground lamb in a large bowl and add the egg mixture, bread crumbs, preserved lemon, pistachios and olives. Mix thoroughly together by hand, and roll into little meatballs.

Place the meatballs on a cookie tray and bake for 10 minutes. To serve, skewer each meatball with a toothpick and place them onto a platter. Drizzle with vin cotto.

WILSON WINERY

There are quesadillas, and then there are Wilson quesadillas – so much more than simply cheese melted inside a tortilla. These quesadillas have complex flavors that come from a slightly spicy corn and zucchini filling (with melted cheese, of course) and are served with a dollop of the corn-zucchini mixture on the side.

1960 Dry Creek Road
Healdsburg, CA 95448
707-433-4355
www.wilsonwinery.com

corn, chile & cheese
QUESADILLAS

chef Donna Parsons

vegi

Pair with Wilson Dry Creek Vally Zinfandel

SERVES 6-8

5 tablespoons vegetable oil

1 cup fresh, mild chiles, small dice

1-1/2 cups zucchini, small dice

kosher salt and freshly ground black pepper

1 cup fresh corn kernels (from 2 medium ears)

1/8 teaspoon chipotle chile powder

1 cup tomato, diced

1/4 cup cilantro, chopped

1 tablespoon fresh lime juice

4 9-inch flour tortillas

2 cups Monterey Jack cheese, grated

sour cream for serving (optional)

Preheat oven to 200°. Fit a rack over a baking sheet and put the sheet in the oven.

Heat 1 tablespoon of the oil in a 12-inch skillet over medium-high heat. Add the chiles and cook, stirring, until they're soft, 3 to 4 minutes. Add the zucchini, season with salt and pepper, and cook, stirring, until the squash softens and starts to brown, 3 to 4 minutes.

Stir in the corn and chipotle powder and cook for 2 minutes. Spoon the mixture into a bowl and let it cool for a few minutes. Then fold in the tomato, cilantro and lime juice. Season to taste with salt and pepper, and set aside 3/4 cup of the mixture.

Place several layers of paper towels on a work surface. Wipe out the skillet, place it on the stovetop over medium-high heat, and add 1 tablespoon of oil. When the oil is hot, place 1 tortilla in the pan. Quickly distribute 1/2 cup of cheese evenly over one half of the tortilla, and about a quarter of the remaining vegetable mixture over the other half. When the underside of the tortilla is browned, use tongs to fold the cheese side over the vegetable side. Place the quesadilla on the paper towels, blot the surface for a few seconds, and then move it to the rack in the oven to keep the quesadilla warm while you cook the rest.

Cut the quesadillas into wedges and serve with the reserved vegetable mixture and sour cream.

SOUPS

Alderbrook Old Barn Zinfandel Chili

White Bean & Sausage Cassoulet

Pasta e Fagioli

Harvest Ribollita with Farro & Olio Nuovo

Braised Lamb Lentil Soup

New England Clam Chowder

Thai Tom Yum Soup

Kramer's Mulligatawny Soup

Celery Root Soup with New Potato Duck Confit Salad

Sausage, Kale & White Bean Soup

Caldo Verde (Grandma's Azorean Kale Soup)

Tortilla Soup

Tuscan White Bean Soup

Simply Delicious Truffled Potato Leek Soup

Crab Bisque with Fennel

Autumn Rock Shrimp Corn Chowder

Lobster Chardonnay Bisque with Meyer Lemon Oil

ALDERBROOK WINERY

Start this recipe one day ahead by soaking the beans overnight. If you use vegetable stock, this becomes a hearty vegetarian chili that is sure to please meat-lovers as well.

2306 Magnolia Drive
Healdsburg, CA 95448
707-433-5987
www.alderbrook.com

alderbrook old barn
ZINFANDEL CHILI

chef Ken Rochioli, K R Catering

Pair with Alderbrook Old Barn Dry Creek Valley Zinfandel

SERVES 4 AS A MAIN COURSE

1 pound (2 cups) small navy
  beans, soaked
1/4 cup olive oil
1 large onion, finely diced
3 small dried red chiles, seeded
15 garlic cloves, minced
1 tablespoon sweet paprika
1/4 teaspoon freshly ground
  black pepper
4 teaspoons ground cumin
6 ounces canned tomato paste
2 tomatoes, coarsely chopped
7 cups or vegetable stock
2 cups Alderbook Old Barn
  Zinfandel
2 bay leaves
1/8 teaspoon cayenne or to
  taste
10 sprigs flat-leaf parsley, tied
  with cotton string
2-1/2 teaspoons salt
10 sprigs flat-leaf parsley,
  minced
10 sprigs cilantro, minced

In a large soup pot over medium-high heat, heat the oil and cook the onion, stirring occasionally, until tender, 6 to 8 minutes. Add the chiles, garlic, paprika, pepper and cumin. Cook, stirring, for 2 to 3 minutes.

Add the tomato paste and cook, stirring, until the mixture thickens, 1 to 2 minutes. Stir in the tomatoes and 1 cup of the broth, and bring the mixture to a boil. Add the beans, the remaining 6 cups of stock, Zinfandel, bay leaves, cayenne and the tied parsley sprigs. Lower the heat to low, cover, and cook the beans until they're tender, 1 to 2 hours.

Before serving, discard the chiles, bay leaves and the tied parsley. Season with salt, and stir in the minced parsley and cilantro.

CLOS DU BOIS

This recipe uses the quick-soak method for preparing the beans. You can also soak the beans overnight in cold water. Serve a crusty baguette with the cassoulet.

19410 Geyserville Avenue
Geyserville, CA 95441
800-222-3189
www.closdubois.com

white bean & sausage
CASSOULET

Pair with Clos du Bois Old Vine Zinfandel

SERVES 6

2 pounds dried Great Northern beans

1 pound bulk chicken-apple sausage

1 onion, whole

1 carrot, whole

4 sprigs thyme

6 bay leaves

2 tablespoons olive oil

½ pound thick-sliced center-cut bacon, cut into 2-inch pieces

1 onion, diced

2 carrots, sliced ¼-inch thick

10 cloves garlic, chopped

1 pound kielbasa, sliced ½-inch thick

2 cups red wine

2 cups beef broth

4 tablespoons tomato paste

1 tablespoon salt

2 teaspoons black pepper

Preheat oven to 375°.

Rinse the beans well and put them in a large stockpot. Add water to cover the beans by 2 inches and place the pot over high heat. Bring the water to a boil for 2 minutes. Remove the pot from the heat, cover, and let it stand for 1 hour. Spread the chicken-apple sausage on a baking sheet and place it in the oven for 15 to 20 minutes. Remove the sausage from the oven and let it cool (it may not be fully cooked through, but that's OK). Add the whole onion, whole carrot, 2 of the thyme sprigs and 3 of the bay leaves to the beans. Add more water to the pot to cover the beans by 2 inches. Bring the pot to a boil, lower the heat and simmer the beans until they're mostly tender, yet still with some bite to them, about 50 to 60 minutes. The beans will have soaked up all most all of the cooking liquid. Meanwhile, pour the olive oil into a large skillet and warm it over medium heat. Add the bacon and cook, stirring every now and then, until the bacon is crispy, about 2 to 3 minutes. Using a slotted spoon, remove the crispy bacon pieces to a paper-towel-lined plate and set aside. To the same skillet, add the diced onion, sliced carrots and garlic, and sweat the mixture for 20 minutes, until the onion begins to turn translucent. Slice the kielbasa on the bias into ½-inch-thick pieces and add them to the vegetable mix. Add the remaining bay leaves and thyme sprigs and cook, stirring, for 5 minutes. Add the wine, beef broth, tomato paste, salt and pepper. Raise the heat to high, bringing the mixture to a boil. Stir well to dissolve the tomato paste and lower the heat. Simmer the mixture for 5 minutes.

Remove the whole onion, whole carrot and the bay leaves from the beans, add the vegetable sausage mixture to the stockpot and return to a low heat. Stir well and cover. Let the cassoulet simmer for 15 to 20 minutes, or until most of the liquid has been absorbed by the beans.

To serve, spoon the cassoulet into individual bowls, sprinkle the top of each serving with some of the reserved crispy bacon, and enjoy.

COPAIN WINES

We use dried cannellini beans in this dish, which must be picked through for stones and soaked overnight in at least 4 inches of water to cover. As a shortcut, you can use 2 16-ounce cans of cannellini beans instead; if you do, use only the chicken stock in this recipe, and omit the water. Farro is a traditional wheat grain eaten in Tuscany; in the United States, it's often labeled as spelt.

7800 Eastside Road
Healdsburg, CA 95448
707-836-8822
www.copainwines.com

PASTA E FAGIOLI
(italian bean stew with farro, herbs & slow roasted pork)

chef Ariel Ross

Pair with Copain Les Voisins Yorkville Highlands Syrah

SERVES 6-8

SOUP

1 tablespoon virgin olive oil

¼ cup pancetta or applewood-smoked bacon, medium dice

1 yellow onion, medium dice

2 stalks celery, medium dice

2 cloves garlic, peeled and smashed with side of chef's knife

1 pinch red pepper flakes

1-½ cups dried cannellini beans, soaked overnight

4 cups homemade chicken stock

3 sprigs fresh thyme

2 bays leaves

5 branches fresh rosemary

1 cup slow-roasted fennel seed-rubbed pork shoulder, gently shredded

sea salt

FARRO

½ cup farro

1 cup water

3 fresh sage leaves

½ teaspoon sea salt or to taste

1 pinch fresh black pepper or to taste

4-6 tablespoons virgin olive oil

½ cup Parmigiano-Reggiano cheese, shaved

smoked Spanish paprika, preferably Chiquilin

Italian flat-leaf parsley leaves for garnish

To prepare the soup, heat the oil in a medium pot over medium heat. Add the pancetta or bacon and sauté, stirring often, until the pork is barely golden brown and some fat has been rendered.

Add the onion and celery and stir to combine. Sauté the mixture until the onions are slightly soft, and add the garlic and red pepper flakes. Cook for 1 to 2 minutes. Drain the beans from the water and add them to the pot, along with the thyme, bay leaves and rosemary (pick out the herbs later if you want a more refined looking soup). Add the chicken stock and 4 cups of water.

Bring the soup to a gentle simmer and cook, uncovered, for about 1-1/2 hours, or until the beans are tender (about 30 minutes for canned beans). Make sure the liquid does not fall below the level of the beans during cooking. If it does, add more water. When the beans are tender, add the cooked meat and simmer for another 5 to 10 minutes to allow the flavors to combine. Season with salt and pepper if necessary.

To cook the farro, combine the first 5 ingredients in a medium pot. Bring the grain to gentle simmer and cook, uncovered, until almost all the water has evaporated, about 25 minutes. The farro should be soft to the bite.

To serve, place a ladle of soup in each bowl. Place a large spoonful of farro in the middle of the soup. Drizzle with olive oil, sprinkle on 1 tablespoon of cheese and a large pinch of the paprika per bowl. Finish with a parsley leaf as garnish.

DAVERO WINERY

Cold weather and a hearty hot soup topped with a float of "new oil" paired with a deep and fruity glass of wine is a treat we look forward to every autumn. The fruit of the orchard and vineyard remind us of the cycle and the joy of life. The ingredients are not set in stone; if you like more or less of something, feel free to adjust. Cubes of winter squash are a great addition to this recipe.

766 Westside Road
Healdsburg, CA 95448
707-431-8000
www.davero.com

HARVEST RIBOLLITA
with farro & olio nuovo

chef Colleen McGlynn

Pair with DaVero Rosso di Bea

SERVES 6-8

2 cups dried white beans

1 cup farro

ham bone, bacon rind, 4 ounces slab bacon (cubed) or pork shin bone

2 or 3 dried chiles

1 onion, diced

4 peeled garlic cloves, minced

1 branch fresh rosemary, leaves chopped

several sprigs fresh thyme, chopped

5 sage leaves, chopped

2 carrots, peeled and sliced

4 ribs celery, sliced

2 leeks, white part only, cleaned and sliced

1 bunch kale, broccoli rabe or chard, cut into ribbons

8 ounces plum tomatoes, chopped

1 large potato, peeled and cubed

kosher salt and pepper

DaVero olive oil

Parmesan cheese for finishing

Cover the beans with several inches of water and let them soak overnight. Drain the beans the next morning.

If you are using whole farro, soak the grain overnight and proceed with the recipe. If you are using "perlato" – semi-pearled or hulled farro – it requires no pre-soaking.

Put the soaked beans in a large pot and cover with fresh water to several inches above the surface. Add the meat and dried chiles. Cook for about 1 hour, until the beans start to soften. Skim off any foam.

Sauté the onion, garlic and herbs over a low flame until they're soft. Add them and the remaining vegetables, along with the farro, to the pot of beans. Add a good pinch of salt. Bring the mixture to a boil and simmer gently for another 30 to 45 minutes, until everything has softened; occasionally skim off any foam and discard it. If the soup becomes too thick, add hot water as needed. Taste and adjust the seasoning with salt and pepper. Discard the bones and rinds, if used.

Serve in a bowl with a swirl of new olive oil (olio nuovo) and a grating of Parmesan, with grilled bread alongside.

DUTCHER CROSSING WINERY

This is no ordinary lentil soup. The long, slow braising of the lamb gives the meat and pan juices incredible depth of flavor, which is passed on to the lentils. This soup is hearty enough to be a main course on a chilly fall or winter evening.

8533 Dry Creek Road
Healdsburg, CA 95448
707-431-2700
www.dutchercrossingwinery.com

braised
LAMB LENTIL SOUP

chef Amber Balshaw, Preferred Sonoma Caterers

Pair with Dutcher Crossing Cabernet Sauvignon

MAKES 2.5 GALLONS

LAMB

1 leg of lamb, approximately 6 lbs
salt and pepper to taste
1/4 cup olive oil
1 pound yellow onions, cut into
   chunks
1 pound carrots, cut into chunks
1 bunch celery, cut into chunks
1 sprig rosemary
6 cloves garlic, crushed
2 cups red wine
water to cover

SOUP

braised lamb leg (see recipe)
1/4 cup olive oil
1 pound onions, diced
1 pound carrots, diced
1 pound celery, diced
2 teaspoons garlic, minced
1 teaspoon cumin
1 teaspoon dried thyme
3 bay leaves
1 pound lentils, rinsed
2 gallons stock (the lamb cooking
   juice plus enough water to get
   2 gallons)

Preheat oven to 250°.

To prepare the braised lamb, cut the leg into 4 large chunks and sprinkle with salt and pepper. In a large Dutch oven, heat the olive oil and brown the lamb pieces on all sides. Add vegetables and herbs, then the wine, and add enough water to cover the ingredients.

Braise the lamb in the oven for 6 to 8 hours, until the meat is tender. Remove the meat and strain, saving the juices (discard the vegetables). Allow the lamb to cool.

To prepare the soup, chop the cooled lamb meat into bite-size pieces. In a large stockpot, add the olive oil and sauté the vegetables, garlic, cumin, thyme and bay leaves over medium heat, until the vegetables are tender.

Add the lentils and stock, and simmer until the lentils are tender, approximately 45 minutes to 1 hour. Remove the bay leaves. Add the lamb and adjust the seasoning with salt and pepper. Heat through, and serve.

DUTTON ESTATE WINERY

A Dutton Estate favorite, this creamy, rich New England-style clam chowder is a classic pairing with a buttery Chardonnay, and does not take long to prepare. Serve the chowder with crusty French bread and a simple green salad, dressed with Meyer lemon vinaigrette, to best complement the wine.

8757 Green Valley Road
Sebastopol, CA 95472
707-829-9463
www.duttonestatewinery.com

new england
CLAM CHOWDER

chef Cynthia Newcomb

Pair with Dutton Estate Kyndall's Reserve Chardonnay

SERVES 6-8

3 8-ounce bottles clam juice

6 6-1/2-ounce cans chopped
  clams, drained, juices
  reserved

1 bay leaf

6 sprigs fresh thyme, tied
  together with cooking twine

1-1/2 pounds russet potatoes,
  peeled and diced

6 slices bacon, cut crosswise
  into 1/2-inch strips

6 tablespoons unsalted butter

2 medium leeks, white and
  light green parts only, halved
  lengthwise and thinly sliced

2 cups onions, diced

1 cup celery, minced

1/3 cup flour

1 cup heavy cream

1 cup milk

1 teaspoon hot pepper sauce,
  if desired

salt and white pepper to taste

Bring the bottled clam juice and drained juices from the clams (but not the clam meat), bay leaf, thyme and potatoes to boil in a heavy large saucepan over high heat. Reduce the heat to medium-low, cover, and simmer until the potatoes are tender, about 10 minutes. Remove from the heat.

Fry the bacon in a large pot over medium heat. Drain the bacon on paper towels, reserving the renderings. Melt the butter with the bacon fat in the pot over medium heat. Add the leeks, onions and celery and sauté them until they're softened, about 10 minutes.

Stir in the flour and cook 2 minutes (do not let the flour brown). Allow to cool slightly. Whisk in the cream and milk. Add the potato mixture, clams and hot pepper sauce, if using. Bring the chowder to a simmer for 2 to 3 minutes to blend the flavors, stirring frequently.

Season to taste with salt and pepper, if necessary. Remove the bay leaf and thyme sprigs before serving.

The chowder can be prepared 1 day ahead. Refrigerate it uncovered until it's cold, then cover the soup and keep it refrigerated. Bring to a simmer before serving.

FORCHINI VINEYARDS & WINERY

Soup is one of our favorite foods during fall and winter, particularly vegetarian versions that help us transition from summer's lighter meals to heavier dishes. This Thai soup, with its sweet and sour flavors and spicy broth, is simple to prepare and comforting to eat. Although bread is not traditionally Thai, a slice of our locally made sourdough bread dipped into the broth is delicious.

5141 Dry Creek Road
Healdsburg, CA 95448
707-431-8886
www.forchini.com

thai
TOM YUM SOUP

vegi

chef Randi Kauppi, Oui Cater

Pair with Forchini Chardonnay or Papa Nonno Tuscan Style Red

SERVES 6

6 cups vegetable stock

2 stalks lemongrass, minced

3 whole kaffir lime leaves
   (available at Asian markets
   and many grocery stores)

2 small red chiles, sliced, or
   1/2 teaspoon red pepper
   flakes

4 cloves garlic, minced

1 thumb-sized piece
   fresh ginger, sliced into
   matchsticks

1 cup fresh mushrooms, sliced

2 cups baby bok choy,
   chopped

1 cup cherry tomatoes

6 ounces coconut milk

1 teaspoon brown sugar

3 tablespoons soy sauce

1 tablespoon fresh lime juice

½ cup fresh basil, chopped

⅓ cup fresh cilantro,
   chopped

Pour the vegetable stock into a soup pot. Add the lemon grass, lime leaves, chiles (or red pepper flakes), garlic and ginger. Bring the mixture to a boil and boil for 5 minutes.

Add the mushrooms, reduce the heat to medium and simmer the mixture for 5 minutes. Add the bok choy and cherry tomatoes, and simmer gently for 2 more minutes; the bok choy should remain crisp. Reduce the heat to low and add the coconut milk, sugar, soy sauce and lime juice.

To serve, ladle the soup into individual bowls and top with the fresh basil and cilantro.

HART'S DESIRE WINES

Mulligatawny is the favorite soup of the "Seinfeld" TV character Kramer (remember the Soup Nazi episode?). To adapt this Indian-spiced dish for meat eaters, add two cups of cooked and diced chicken at the end of the cooking process, and stir through. You can also use chicken stock in place of the vegetable stock.

53 Front Street
Healdsburg, CA 95448
707-433-3097
www.hartsdesirewines.com

kramer's
MULLIGATAWNY SOUP

vegi

chef Evan Euphrat

Pair with Hart's Desire Claude Thomas Vineyard Dry Creek Valley Sauvignon Blanc

SERVES 6

SEASONING

2 ounces coconut oil (more may be needed)

2 tablespoons ginger root, minced

1 sweet onion, minced

5 garlic cloves, minced

2 jalapeño chiles

2 tablespoons curry powder

1/4 teaspoon cloves, ground

1/4 teaspoon cinnamon, ground

1-1/2 teaspoons cumin

1 teaspoon turmeric

SOUP

1 quart vegetable stock, low sodium

2 stalks celery, diced

1 sweet onion, diced

2 carrots, diced

1 Granny Smith apple, peeled, cored and diced

2 potatoes, peeled and diced

1 cup chickpeas

1 cup coconut milk

salt and pepper to taste

1/4 cup parsley, chopped

In a large, heavy-bottom pot, add all of the seasoning ingredients and cook over medium heat, until the onion is translucent and the smell is fragrant. Add additional oil if necessary.

Add the vegetable stock to the same pot and mix well. Follow with the celery, onion, carrots, apple, potatoes and chickpeas, stir, and bring the mixture to a boil. Reduce the heat and simmer the soup for approximately 30 minutes, until the potatoes and chickpeas are cooked through.

Remove the soup from the heat, stir in the coconut milk, and season to taste with salt and pepper. Ladle the soup into bowls and garnish with the parsley.

HARVEST MOON ESTATE & WINERY

Typically, Zinfandels are limited to service with a big piece of meat, but we're excited to present to you a warm winter soup that goes beautifully with our elegant Russian River Valley Zinfandel. This is a go-to recipe when you want something warm in your belly. Enjoy it with good company.

2192 Olivet Road
Santa Rosa, CA 95401
707-573-8711
www.harvestmoonwinery.com

CELERY ROOT SOUP

with new potato duck confit salad & white truffle oil

chef Todd Davies

Pair with Harvest Moon Russian River Valley Zinfandel

SERVES 12

2 bunches leeks, white parts only

2 heads celery root

2 russet potatoes

1/3 cup unsalted butter

6 cups chicken stock

1 bay leaf

salt to taste

1/2 teaspoon white pepper

1/2 cup cream

2 pounds new potatoes

4 legs duck confit (2 pounds total weight)

1 cup sour cream

truffle oil

Slice the leek whites into 1/4-inch rings and immerse them in cold water to remove any dirt. Peel the celery root heads and russet potatoes, and cut them into coarse 1-inch cubes.

In a large pot over medium heat, melt the butter, add the leeks, and cook them until they're translucent. Add the celery root and potatoes and continue cooking for 5 minutes.

Add the chicken stock and bay leaf, and bring the mixture to a boil.

Reduce the heat and simmer until the vegetables are soft. With a hand mixer, puree the vegetables, season with salt and white pepper, and add the cream. Strain the mixture through a fine strainer.

While you are cooking the soup, cook the new potatoes, starting them in a pot of cold salted water and bringing them to a boil over high heat. Cook the potatoes until they're just done, then strain off the water.

Debone the duck confit and coarsely chop the pieces. Slice the new potatoes and add them to the confit. Add the sour cream and stir to combine the ingredients. Season to taste.

Ladle the soup into bowls and garnish with the new potato-duck confit salad. Drizzle some truffle oil over each portion and serve.

LYNMAR ESTATE

There is nothing better than a warm bowl of homemade soup on a cold evening! At Lynmar Estate, we grow many of our own vegetables, with kale being quite prolific. With the creaminess of white beans and the richness of sausage and olive oil, this soup appeals to the earthy core of our Russian River Valley Pinot Noir. Add some crusty sourdough bread and you have a great meal.

3909 Frei Road
Sebastopol, CA 95472
707-829-3374
www.lynmarestate.com

sausage, kale &
WHITE BEAN SOUP

chef David Frakes

Pair with Lynmar Russian River Valley Pinot Noir

SERVES 8

1 cup cannellini or navy white
    beans
1 large bunch kale, rinsed,
    stemmed and chopped
1 tablespoon olive oil
1 pound mild Italian sausage,
    casings removed
1 cup shallots, chopped
4 cups unsalted chicken
    stock
1 large heirloom tomato,
    peeled and cut into 1/4-inch
    dice (or 1 tablespoon
    tomato paste)
salt and pepper to taste
very small pinch red pepper
    flakes (optional)

Place the beans in a large container and cover them with several inches of cool water. Let stand 8 hours or overnight. Drain and rinse the beans before using them

Cook the soaked beans in 6 to 8 cups of water, over a medium boil, for 45 minutes to 1 hour. Do not drain.

Bring a separate pot of salted water to a boil. Add the kale and simmer it until it's bright green and tender, about 2 minutes. Drain the kale in a strainer and rinse with cool running water. Set aside.

In a soup pot, heat the olive oil over medium heat. Brown the sausage completely, using a wooden spoon to crumble it in the pan, about 5 minutes. Remove the sausage from the pot with a slotted spoon and set it aside. Add the shallots to the pot and cook them until they're soft, about 3 minutes, adding a drop more olive oil if needed. Pour in a splash of chicken stock and scrape up any browned bits of sausage in the pot.

Return the sausage to the pot along with the beans and their cooking liquid. Stir in the rest of the chicken broth. Bring the soup to a boil, reduce the heat to low, and simmer it, uncovered, for 15 minutes. Add the kale, tomatoes (or tomato paste) and cook about 4 minutes longer. Season with salt, pepper and red pepper flakes to taste.

RAYMOND BURR VINEYARDS

My grandparents came from four different islands in the Azores. My mother's mother, Maria Simas, came from the village of Sao Roque, which is on the island of Pico. In the islands, neighbors have a way of giving other families colorful nicknames depending on some obvious trait of that family. The ingredients of this Azorean soup were readily available to all, since every yard grew kale, potatoes, onions and garlic – and they all had a pig, which ended up as linguica. So, if you didn't have much else to eat, you could always fall back on this tasty soup. My grandmother and her family must have relied heavily on it, because they were locally known as the Caldo Verdes.

8339 West Dry Creek Road
Geyserville, CA 95441
707-433-8559
www.raymondburrvineyards.com

CALDO VERDE
(grandma's azorean soup)

chef Robert Benevides

Pair with Raymond Burr Vineyards Sonoma County Cabernet Franc

SERVES 4

10 to 12 kale leaves
2 quarts water or broth
1 stick cinnamon
1 bay leaf
1 teaspoon whole allspice
1/2 cup olive oil
1 medium onion, chopped
2 garlic cloves, pressed
1 pound linguica
4 russet potatoes, peeled
   and diced
salt to taste

Cut out and discard the white center spines from the kale. Shred or roll the leaves together and slice them very thin. Add the water or broth to a large pot, place the shredded kale in the pot, and bring to a boil.

Place the cinnamon, bay leaf and allspice in a tea caddy, or tie them in cheesecloth. Add the spices and olive oil to the pot, then add the chopped onion and garlic.

Slice the linguica in 1/4- to 1/2-inch pieces and microwave or fry them. Drain the linguica to eliminate most of the grease, then add the sausage to the boiling kale.

When the kale is almost tender, after approximately 50 minutes, add the diced potatoes and continue cooking for another 20 to 30 minutes. The potatoes should break up and melt into the soup (do not use Yukon Golds). Remove the spices, add salt to taste, and serve the soup with crusty bread.

ROBERT RUE VINEYARD

Quick to fix and full of flavor, this popular soup offers south-of-the border appeal and is a perfect complement to our Robert Rue Estate Wood Road Zinfandel.

1406 Wood Road
Fulton, CA 95439
707-578-1601
www.robertruevineyard.com

TORTILLA SOUP

chef Kathy Bradley

Pair with Robert Rue Vineyard Wood Road Reserve Zinfandel

SERVES 4

4 cups chicken broth

1 cup cornbread mix

2 cups salsa

1 can whole kernel corn

1 can black beans

corn tortilla chips

1 pint sour cream

1 small can sliced black olives,
  drained

In a soup pot, add the dry cornbread mix and chicken broth and whisk to incorporate the ingredients. Add the salsa, corn, black beans and 2 handfuls of crumbled tortilla chips. Bring to a slow boil, reduce the heat, and simmer for approximately 10 minutes.

Ladle the soup into individual serving bowls, top with a dollop of sour cream and sliced olives, and serve with additional tortilla chips.

SBRAGIA FAMILY VINEYARDS

This is one of my very favorite winter soups to have with a loaf of warm, crusty bread and a glass of Sbragia Zin. Enjoy!

9990 Dry Creek Road
Geyserville, CA 95441
707-473-2992
www.sbragia.com

tuscan
WHITE BEAN SOUP

chef Tracy Bidia

Pair with Sbragia Family Vineyards Zinfandel

SERVES 4-6

3 cups dried Great Northern white beans

10 cups water

1/4 cup extra virgin olive oil, with extra for garnish

1 medium yellow onion, diced

1 carrot, diced

1 rib of celery, sliced

6 garlic gloves, minced

2 cups tomatoes, chopped, with their liquid

2-1/2 teaspoons salt

2 quarts chicken stock

1 bunch oregano, chopped

1 bunch of basil, chopped

3 large sprigs rosemary, chopped

Place the cleaned white beans in a large stockpot and cover with 10 cups of water. Bring the beans to a boil, turn off the heat, and let them sit for 1 hour. Drain the beans and set aside.

In a large pot, heat the olive oil over medium heat. Sauté the onion, carrot and celery until they're soft, about 10 minutes. Stir in the garlic and cook about 5 minutes. Add the tomatoes, beans, salt, pepper and chicken stock and cook for 1 hour.

Add the oregano, basil and rosemary and cook for another hour, until the beans are very tender. Garnish with a drizzle of extra virgin olive oil and serve hot.

SHELDON WINES

When the weather starts to get chilly, we turn to this family favorite to warm the belly and the soul. We like the richness and texture of Yukon Gold potatoes, but you can substitute any variety you like.

1301 Cleveland Avenue
Santa Rosa, CA 95401
707-865-6755
www.sheldonwines.com

simply delicious truffled
POTATO LEEK SOUP

chef Dylan Sheldon

vegi

Pair with Sheldon Chardonnay or Pinot Noir

SERVES 4-6

SOUP

3 medium leeks

1 medium yellow onion

3 cloves garlic

4 tablespoons unsalted butter

1 bay leaf

2 sprigs rosemary

4 sprigs thyme

4 medium to large Yukon Gold
   potatoes

1/3 cup dry white wine

3-1/3 cups vegetable broth

1 teaspoon sea salt

1/8 teaspoon ground fennel
   seed

1/8 teaspoon ground black
   pepper

white truffle oil

CHEESE CRISPS

1/4 cup Parmigiano-Reggiano or
   cave-aged Gruyère cheese

rosemary, thyme and cayenne,
   to taste (optional)

To prepare the soup, split the leeks down the middle with a sharp knife and wash them thoroughly to remove any grit. Mince the white parts and the first inch of the light green stalk. Dice the onion. Smash the garlic cloves with the flat side of a chef's knife and chop them.

In a large stockpot over low heat, melt the butter with the leeks, onion, garlic, bay leaf, rosemary and thyme. Simmer the mixture on low for about 5 minutes, until the vegetables are soft but not caramelized.

Meanwhile, wash and dice the potatoes. Add the potatoes, wine and vegetable broth to the leek mixture, turn the heat to medium and stir for 3 to 5 minutes. Turn the heat down to low and add the sea salt, ground fennel and black pepper. Simmer on low heat until the vegetables are tender, about 15 to 20 minutes.

To prepare the cheese crisps, grate about 1/4 cup of cheese. In a non-stick pan over medium-low heat, drop clusters of grated cheese into the pan; you want each to be the size and shape of a potato chip. The cheese will melt and blister into medallions that can be scraped off with a spatula into 'cheese chips'. Set the chips aside on a plate, giving them a very light sprinkle of rosemary, thyme cayenne, if desired.

To serve, remove the bay leaf, rosemary and thyme from the soup and puree it in a blender until it's smooth and creamy. Pour the soup into bowls and garnish each with a few drops of white truffle oil and a cheese crisp.

SONOMA-CUTRER

This is a wonderful recipe that works very well with the full range of Chardonnays we make at Sonoma-Cutrer. Each wine brings out a different characteristic in the bisque. You can make the soup a day ahead; it will develop a fuller flavor if it's allowed to rest for a day.

4401 Slusser Road
Windsor, CA 95492
707-237-3489
www.sonomacutrer.com

CRAB BISQUE
with fennel

chef Bruce Riezenman, Park Avenue Catering

Pair with Sonoma-Cutrer Russian River Ranches Chardonnay

SERVES 8

2 tablespoons olive oil

2 cups yellow onion, finely diced

1 cup leeks, white part and light green only, washed and cut into thin rings

2 tablespoons garlic

$\frac{1}{2}$ teaspoon fennel seed

$\frac{1}{4}$ teaspoon serrano chile, minced

$\frac{1}{4}$ teaspoon red pepper flakes

salt and pepper to taste

$\frac{1}{2}$ cup Sonoma-Cutrer Chardonnay

4 ears fresh corn, removed from the cobs; reserve "corn milk" and cobs

3 cups crab (or chicken) broth

1 cup fennel bulb, thinly sliced

$\frac{1}{3}$ cup white rice

1-$\frac{1}{2}$ teaspoons lemon zest

2 cups coconut milk

1 pound Dungeness crab meat

2 teaspoons extra virgin olive oil

minced chives, for garnish

Place the olive oil in a large saucepan. Allow it to pre-heat for 30 seconds. Add the onions, leeks, garlic, fennel seed, chile and red pepper flakes. Cook the mixture until the vegetables are soft but not browned. Season with salt and pepper, add the Chardonnay, and simmer for 5 minutes, uncovered.

In a separate saucepan, add the corn cobs and the broth. Cook covered for 10 to 15 minutes. Strain and save the broth. Add the corn/chicken broth to the vegetable/Chardonnay mix and simmer. Add the corn, fennel bulb slices, rice and lemon zest. Simmer for 30 minutes, until the rice is fully cooked and soft. Add the coconut milk and simmer for 5 minutes.

Puree in a blender and strain the soup so that you have a fine and smooth consistency. If the soup is too thick, add additional broth. Taste and season with salt and pepper.

When ready to serve, bring the bisque to a simmer and gently fold in 3/4 of the crab meat. Serve the soup in warm bowls topped with the remaining crab meat, a drizzle of olive oil and a sprinkling of chives.

WHITE OAK VINEYARDS & WINERY

Local chef Dan Lucia, friend and neighbor of White Oak Vineyards & Winery, created this dish to complement our Russian River Valley Chardonnay. Enjoy this warm autumn chowder with herbed crudités as you relax and embrace the colors of the new season.

7505 Highway 128
Healdsburg, CA 95448
707-433-8429
www.whiteoakwinery.com

ROCK SHRIMP CORN CHOWDER

chef Dan Lucia , DL Catering

Pair with White Oak Russian River Valley Chardonnay

SERVES 6-8

⅓ cup local olive oil
½ cup yellow onion, diced
½ cup red onion, diced
4 tablespoons garlic,
　chopped
1 cup celery, diced
½ cup leeks, sliced
4 cups white corn kernels
8 cups chicken stock
1 cup heavy whipping cream
1 pound dry-cured bacon,
　diced
½ cup flour
4 tablespoons canola oil
1 pound fresh rock shrimp
salt and pepper to taste
½ cup crème fraiche
⅓ cup cilantro, chopped

In a stockpot, heat the olive oil on medium heat. Add the onions and sauté them for 5 to 6 minutes, until they start to turn translucent. Add the garlic, celery, leeks and corn kernels, and cook for 8 to 10 minutes, until the ingredients are soft and tender. Add the chicken stock and cream, and bring to a simmer.

In a separate pan, render the bacon until it's crispy. Strain the bacon fat into a sauté pan. Heat the bacon fat and add the flour. Stir the mixture until it becomes light brown and has thickened. Add the rendered bacon and the bacon fat/flour roux to the soup base. Stir until the chowder has thickened.

Heat the canola oil in a sauté pan and add the rock shrimp. Season with salt and pepper and cook briefly, stirring, for about 15 seconds. Add the shrimp to the chowder.

To serve, ladle the soup into bowls and garnish with a dollop of crème fraiche and a sprinkling of cilantro.

WINDSOR OAKS VINEYARDS & WINERY

This is a wine country version of the classic Maine lobster bisque. You can order lobster and shrimp shells from seafood markets.

10810 Hillview Road
Windsor, CA 95492
707-433-4050
www.windsoroaksvineyards.com

LOBSTER CHARDONNAY BISQUE
with meyer lemon oil

chef Matt Paille

Pair with Windsor Oaks Vineyards Reserve Chardonnay

SERVES 10

LOBSTER STOCK

½ gallon cold water
2-½ pounds lobster shells
½ pound shrimp shells
2 carrots, peeled and diced
1 large yellow onion, finely diced
1 bay leaf
1 bunch thyme
3 long celery stalks, diced into ¼-inch pieces

BISQUE

½ cup shallots, diced
6 cloves garlic, minced
¼ cup butter
½ bottle Windsor Oaks Reserve Chardonnay
1 12-ounce can San Marzano whole tomatoes, drained
½ gallon heavy cream
½ gallon lobster stock (see recipe)
1 tablespoon flour
½ pound lobster meat, finely chopped
1 ounce lemon juice
salt to taste
small dash red pepper flakes to taste
DaVero Meyer lemon oil
chives, for garnish

To prepare the stock, preheat the oven to 400°. Roast the lobster and shrimp shells for 10 to 12 minutes, until they're well caramelized.

Add all the ingredients to a 2-gallon stockpot and let the mixture simmer gently for 30 minutes. Skim off the foam off and strain the stock through a fine-mesh strainer; discard the solids.

To prepare the bisque, in a 2-gallon stockpot, sweat the shallots and garlic in the butter, until the vegetables are just translucent, about 5 minutes. Add the wine and simmer until the liquid is reduced by two thirds.

Over medium heat, add the drained tomatoes and thoroughly mash them and stir with a wooden spoon. Cook for 10 minutes. Add the cream and lobster stock together, and simmer another 10 minutes.

Take a small pat of butter and mix it into the flour. Add this to the soup and stir well; simmer 5 minutes more. Remove the pot from the heat, and using an immersion blender, puree the bisque until it's smooth. Strain through a fine-mesh strainer and discard the solids.

Add the lobster meat and the lemon juice, and return the soup to a simmer. Adjust the seasoning if necessary.

Before serving, garnish the bisque with a light drizzle of the Meyer lemon oil and chopped chives.

SALADS & SIDES

Warm Lentil Salad with Bacon

Tartiflette au Reblochon

Potato & Ham Gratin with Truffle Oil

The Wedge with Blue Goddess Dressing

Roasted Golden Beet Salad

Russian River Harvest Chicken Salad

Tuna & White Bean Salad

Nancy's Ambrosia Fruit Salad with Anise & Muscat Canelli

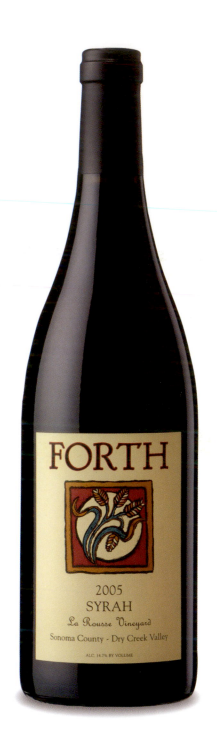

FORTH VINEYARDS

This is a most delicious and versatile dish. By itself, it's a wonderful accompaniment to grilled fish, lamb and beef. With a poached or fried egg on top, it's a healthy and tasty main course. Or simply enjoy it just as it is.

4791 Dry Creek Road
Healdsburg, CA 95448
707-473-0553
www.familywines.com

WARM LENTIL SALAD
with bacon

chef Jann Forth

Pair with Forth La Rousse Vineyard Dry Creek Valley Syrah

SERVES 6

SALAD

3 slices thickly cut bacon

1 clove garlic, peeled and sliced

1 cup yellow onion, diced

1 stalk celery, cut into 1-inch
   pieces

3 cups water

8 ounces French green lentils,
   picked through, rinsed and
   drained

2 teaspoons fresh thyme,
   chopped

¼ cup red onion, diced

¼ cup celery, diced

¼ cup Italian flat leaf parsley,
   chopped

DRESSING

2 tablespoons red wine vinegar

1 tablespoon Dijon mustard

½ teaspoon kosher salt

freshly ground pepper
   to taste (start with ¼
   teaspoon)

¼ cup olive oil

Place the bacon in a cold sauté pan on the stove. Turn on to medium heat. This will both render the fat and cook the bacon. Cook the bacon until it is crisp. Remove the slices with a slotted spoon and set them on paper towels to drain.

Sauté the garlic, onion and celery in the bacon drippings in the pan, until all are tender and slightly translucent. Add the water, lentils and thyme. Bring to a boil, cover and reduce the heat to a simmer for 30 minutes, or until the lentils are tender.

While the lentils are cooking, make the dressing. Whisk together the red wine vinegar, mustard, kosher salt and freshly ground pepper. Add the olive oil and whisk again.

Drain the lentils and toss them with the dressing in a bowl, while the lentils are still warm. Let the lentils cool at room temperature for about 30 minutes. Once the salad is cool, add the red onion, celery and parsley, and serve.

HOBO WINE COMPANY

Tartiflette is a casserole native to the French alps, and Reblochon (ruh-blow-SHON), a creamy cow's milk cheese, is the only type used by the locals. The French typically add lardons – strips of pork fat – or bacon to the casserole, but this is a vegetarian version. It's just as delicious, and we can serve it to everyone.

132 Plaza Street
Healdsburg, CA 95448
707-473-0337
www.hobowines.com

TARTIFLETTE
au Reblochon

chef Lynn Wheeler

vegi

Pair with Folk Machine Central Coast Pinot Noir

SERVES 6

3 large, evenly sized Yukon Gold potatoes

1 tablespoon butter

1 large onion, sliced

¼ cup dry white wine

2 tablespoons crème fraiche

1 round (8 ounces) Reblochon cheese

salt and pepper to taste

Preheat oven to 425°.

Bring a large pot of salted water to a boil over high heat. Add the potatoes, and gently boil them for 20 minutes. Do not overcook. Drain the potatoes and let them cool a few minutes.

While they're still warm, peel the potatoes with your fingers, and cut them into slices about ⅓-inch thick.

Grease an 8-inch-square baking dish.

Melt the butter in a frying pan and add the onion. Cook and stir until the onions are translucent, about 5 minutes. Add the wine, and simmer the mixture until most of the wine has evaporated. Remove the pan from the heat.

Place half of the potatoes in the prepared baking dish, and spread half of the onions over the potatoes. Layer in the remaining potatoes, then spread the crème fraiche over them. Add the remaining half of the onions.

Cut the Reblochon into thin slices, and layer the slices evenly over the top of the casserole. Bake until the cheese is melted and a bit brown, about 15 minutes. Season to taste with salt and pepper, and serve hot.

HOLDREDGE WINES

The white truffle oil that finishes this hearty gratin is the perfect flavor bridge to the earthy, savory character of our Pinot Noir.

51 Front Street
Healdsburg, CA 95448
707-431-1424
www.holdredge.com

POTATO & HAM GRATIN
with truffle oil

chef Bruce Riezenman, Park Avenue Catering

Pair with Holdredge Selection Massale Russian River Valley Pinot Noir

SERVES 8

4 pounds russet potatoes, peeled

2 tablespoons butter

½ pound of 1-year sharp white cheddar cheese, grated

½ pound fontina cheese, grated

½ pound applewood-smoked ham, thinly sliced, cut in julienne strips

6 leaves fresh sage, minced

4 cloves garlic, minced

1-½ cups heavy cream

½ teaspoon kosher salt

¼ teaspoon white pepper

2 tablespoons white truffle oil

Preheat oven to 350°.

Butter a 12-inch by 8-inch by 2.5-inch oval casserole dish.

Thinly slice the potatoes. Combine all the ingredients except for the truffle oil in a large mixing bowl, and place the mixture in the casserole. Press it down with a spatula so the potatoes are just covered with the cream. If needed, add additional cream so that the level comes almost to the top, but does not quite cover, all the potatoes.

Bake the gratin for 1 hour, or until a small knife run through the center passes without resistance. Allow the dish to rest for 20 minutes, drizzle the top lightly with truffle oil, and serve warm.

For an alternate presentation, allow the cooked gratin to cool, press down to compress it slightly and refrigerate overnight. Once it's chilled, cut the gratin into squares and bake for 10 to 15 minutes in a buttered baking pan (at 375°) until the gratin is crusty on the outside and warm inside. Drizzle lightly with white truffle oil and serve.

J. RICKARDS WINERY

The iceberg wedge salad has become trendy again, and the Rickards family enjoys it with a variety of dressings and toppings. When I tried this recipe the first time, the blue cheese and oils gave the salad the creamy texture associated with the mayonnaise-based Green Goddess dressing, hence the "Blue" name. There are no limits to the variations you can try with toppings. At our table, crisp bacon pieces often show up, sometimes our own walnuts, roasted and chopped. But the secret ingredient is our Sauvignon Blanc, which offsets the lemon juice and rice vinegar just enough to balance the pungency of the cheese.

24505 Chianti Road
Cloverdale, CA 95425
707-758-3441
www.jrwinery.com

THE WEDGE
with blue goddess dressing

chef Eliza Rickards

vegi

Pair with J. Rickards Alexander Valley Sauvignon Blanc

SERVES 6

SALAD

1 head iceberg lettuce,
   cut into 6 wedges, core
   removed
1 large tomato, diced
½ cup chopped hazelnuts,
   lightly toasted
1 cup crumbled blue cheese

DRESSING

2 tablespoons rice vinegar
1 tablespoon fresh lemon
   juice
1 tablespoon J. Rickards
   Sauvignon Blanc
½ cup extra virgin olive oil
½ cup roasted walnut oil
½ cup crumbled blue cheese
¼ teaspoon salt
¼ teaspoon freshly ground
   black pepper

To prepare the dressing, in a small bowl, whisk together the vinegar, lemon juice, wine and the two oils. Add the blue cheese and mash it with the whisk to break it up (I use an electric emulsifier). Season with salt and pepper.

To assemble the salad, place the lettuce wedges on a serving plate. Drizzle 3 to 4 tablespoons of the dressing over each wedge and then layer the tomato, nuts and blue cheese on top. Enjoy!

KORBEL CHAMPAGNE CELLARS

Roasted beets add a hearty character to this delicious fall salad, and Point Reyes Blue Cheese adds a tangy note and creaminess – perfect for the effervescence of our Le Premier bubbly.

13250 River Road
Guerneville, CA 95446
707-824-7000
www.korbel.com

roasted

GOLDEN BEET SALAD

with pears, arugula & point reyes blue cheese

chef Robin Lehnhoff-McCray

Pair with Korbel Le Premier

SERVES 6-8

SALAD

2 pounds golden beets

2 large d'Anjou pears

2 cups young arugula

4 ounces Point Reyes Blue Cheese, crumbled

DRESSING

½ cup white balsamic vinegar

1 tablespoon whole-grain mustard

¼ teaspoon red pepper flakes

1 tablespoon fresh oregano, chopped

½ teaspoon kosher salt

¼ teaspoon black pepper

1 cup extra virgin olive oil

Preheat oven to 375°

To prepare the dressing, in a small bowl combine all the ingredients except for the oil. Whisk in the oil and set aside.

Place the beets in a shallow roasting pan with 1 cup of water. Cover with foil and roast for 1 hour, or until the beets are tender. When they're cool enough to handle, peel the beets and cut them into bite-size wedges.

Add the dressing to the beets, and then core and slice the pears. Immediately toss the pears into the dressed beets to prevent them from discoloring. Toss in the arugula and blue cheese. Season the salad with more salt and pepper, if necessary, and serve immediately.

MICHAEL BERNARD WINES

This recipe is a combination of my grandma's famous curry dip and a salad we would have at our favorite place for lunch. At a family lunch, Grandma would be the first to suggest a great glass of Chardonnay with this salad. Cheers to you Grandma!

779 Westside Road
Healdsburg, CA 95448
707-433-2900
www.michaelbernardwines.com

HARVEST CHICKEN SALAD

chef Christine Cureton

Pair with Michael Bernard Orsi Vineyard Russian River Valley Chardonnay

SERVES 4

4 chicken breasts, cooked
   and chopped
1 can water chestnuts,
   slivered
1/4 cup dried cranberries
1/4 cup green onion, diced
mayonnaise, just enough to
   bind together
1-1/2 teaspoons curry powder
1 teaspoon garlic powder
salt and pepper to taste

Combine all the ingredients in a bowl and mix well. Serve on a bed of butter lettuce with homemade pita chips. You can also stuff the salad into fresh pita pockets.

PHILIP STALEY VINEYARDS

This is a recipe I've been making and reinventing for years. The original was handwritten on a piece of paper and its origin is long forgotten. I modified the dish years ago by adding the tuna, and have served it as a main course ever since. It's one of our favorite recipes for an outdoor summer lunch or dinner.

4791 Dry Creek Road
Healdsburg, CA 95448
707-486-0746
www.familywines.com

tuna &
WHITE BEAN SALAD

chef Pam Staley

Pair with Philip Staley Russian River Valley Viognier

SERVES 4-6

SALAD

2 cans (3 cups) cannellini
  beans, rinsed and drained
1 cup roasted red pepper,
  chopped
10 oil-cured black olives,
  pitted and rough chopped
2 tablespoons red onion,
  finely chopped
1/2 teaspoon fresh rosemary,
  chopped
1 cup fennel, thinly sliced
2 cans (12 ounces) Italian tuna
  in olive oil, drained
2 tablespoons Italian parsley,
  coarsely chopped

DRESSING

6 tablespoons extra virgin
  olive oil
2 cloves garlic, peeled and
  cut into thin slivers
6 tablespoons fresh lemon
  juice
sea salt to taste

In a large bowl, mix the drained beans, roasted red pepper, olives, onion and rosemary. Mound the bean mixture on a platter or in a large shallow bowl. Place the fennel slices around the beans.

Break up the tuna and spread it over the beans. Sprinkle the Italian parsley over the top. Add freshly ground black pepper to taste.

To prepare the dressing, in a small sauté pan, combine the oil and garlic and cook over low heat until the garlic is golden. Turn off the heat and add the lemon juice. Add sea salt to taste. Stir the dressing and let it rest until it's tepid.

Pour the dressing over the salad and bring it to the table. Toss and serve immediately.

STEPHEN & WALKER WINERY

With the year-long availability of fresh fruit in Sonoma County, there is no need to even think about using canned fruit cocktail in this refreshing salad. Just about any firm-flesh, in-season fresh fruit can be used, including pineapple, strawberries, cherries, clementines, peaches, nectarines, pears, kiwifruit and, of course, grapes.

243 Healdsburg Avenue
Healdsburg, CA 95448
707-431-8749
www.trustwine.com

nancy's
AMBROSIA FRUIT SALAD
with anise & muscat canelli

chef Nancy Walker

Pair with Stephen & Walker Patrona Muscat Canelli

SERVES 16

1-1/2 cups water
1-1/4 cups sugar
3 tablespoons lemon juice
2 tablespoons aniseed
1/2 teaspoon salt
1/2 cup Stephen & Walker Patrona Muscat Canelli, chilled
12 cups assorted fresh fruit

In a small saucepan, combine the water, sugar, lemon juice, aniseed and salt, and bring the mixture to a boil. Reduce the heat and simmer, uncovered, for 15 minutes. Remove the pan from the heat, cover it and refrigerate until the mixture is chilled.

Add the Muscat Canelli to the chilled sugar mixture. Strain the syrup and discard the aniseed.

Place the fruit in a large bowl; add the syrup and toss to coat. Cover the bowl and refrigerate until you're ready to serve.

PASTA & RICE

Rigatoni & Meatballs

Cabernet Braised Angus Beef Sugo Ziti

Rigatoni Salsiccia

Italian Sausage Ragu with Penne

Lemon Risotto with Shrimp

Mac & Cheese with Bacon

Red Pepper, Spinach & Goat Cheese Ravioli

Sausage Arrabbiata & Dolcetto

Smoked Wild Boar Bolognese

Pumpkin Gnocchi with Gorgonzola Cream

FRANCIS FORD COPPOLA WINERY

This is one of the most popular menu items at RUSTIC, Francis's Favorites, our full-service restaurant. It comes from Francis Ford Coppola's "personal pantheon" of traditional Italian recipes.

300 Via Archimedes
Geyserville, CA 95441
707-857-1485
www.franciscoppolawinery.com

RIGATONI & MEATBALLS

Pair with Francis Ford Coppola Alexander Valley Director's Cut Cabernet Sauvignon

MAKES 16 LARGE MEATBALLS

MEATBALLS

1 pound ground veal
1 pound ground pork
1 pound ground beef
5 eggs
2 tablespoons garlic, chopped
1 cup yellow onions, minced
1/2 cup parsley, chopped
3/4 cup Parmesan, grated
1-1/2 cups bread crumbs
1/2 teaspoon crushed red pepper flakes
3 teaspoons ground black pepper
2 tablespoons kosher salt
1/4 cup olive oil for frying

TOMATO SAUCE

4 28-ounce cans whole tomatoes
2 cups yellow onion, chopped
2 bunches fresh basil

2 pounds rigatoni pasta

Preheat oven to 350°.

To prepare the meatballs, mix all the ingredients except for the oil. Form the meat mixture into tennis ball-sized balls. Add the oil to a frying pan, preferably one large enough to cook the sauce (see below). When the oil is hot, add the meatballs and brown them on all sides. Remove and set aside.

To prepare the sauce, drain the juice from the tomatoes and reserve the liquid in a bowl. In another bowl, hand-crush the tomatoes until they are in coarse chunks, and set aside.

In the pan used to cook the meatballs, add the onions and sauté on medium-low heat until they're translucent, about 20 minutes. Then add the crushed tomatoes to the pan and cook for 10 minutes more on medium heat. Add one-third of the liquid from the tomatoes and one-third of the fresh basil. Cook for 15 minutes. Using the same method, add the remaining tomato and basil in batches. When the last batch has been added and cooked for 15 minutes, the sauce is complete.

Into a large baking dish, pour half of the sauce. Add the meatballs and pour more sauce over them, until the sauce reaches halfway up the meatballs (you will have some leftover). Bake for 1 hour.

Meanwhile, cook the rigatoni according to the package directions and drain. Make sure the pasta is cooked al dente, or firm to the bite. Mix the remaining sauce with the cooked rigatoni, and place the meatballs on top, and spoon the baked sauce over the meatballs. Serve.

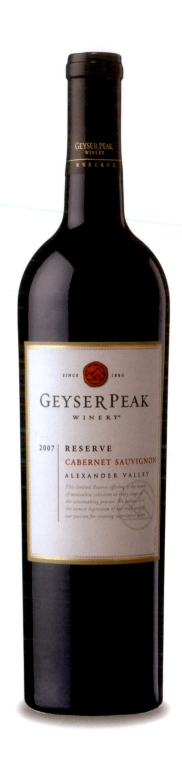

GEYSER PEAK WINERY

After all the hard work of harvest is over, and the evenings begin to cool with the anticipation of winter, this is the perfect warm and hearty dish to celebrate the beauty of nature and the fruit of the Cabernet Sauvignon vine. Sugo is Italian for a "long-simmered sauce;" the extra time it takes to simmer means extra flavor.

22281 Chianti Road
Geyserville, CA 95441
707-857-9400
www.geyserpeakwinery.com

cabernet braised

ANGUS BEEF SUGO ZITI

chef Tim Vallery, Peloton Catering

Pair with Geyser Peak Cabernet Sauvignon

SERVES 12

2 tablespoons olive oil

1-1/2 pounds certified Angus top sirloin, cut into 3/4-inch dice

1 tablespoon granulated garlic

2 teaspoons black pepper, freshly ground

1 tablespoon kosher salt

1 cup shallot, minced

1/4 cup fresh garlic, minced

1 bottle Geyser Peak Cabernet Sauvignon

1 bunch fresh thyme, tied with butcher's twine

2 bay leaves

45 ounces canned stewed tomatoes

1-1/2 teaspoons dried oregano

1 quart low-sodium beef broth

salt and pepper to taste

1 pound ziti pasta

Parmesan or dry jack cheese, shaved

Italian flat-leaf parsley, chopped

Preheat a heavy-bottom sauté pan. Season the meat with the salt, granulated garlic and pepper. Add the olive oil to the pan and brown the meat. Add the shallot and garlic and cook, stirring, until they're translucent.

Deglaze the pan with the Cabernet Sauvignon. Place the meat and deglazed mixture into a saucepan. Add the thyme bunch and bay leaves. Reduce the mixture by one-half (approximately 30 minutes). Add the tomatoes and dried oregano, and continue to cook for an additional 10 minutes. Add the beef broth and simmer for 2 to 3 hours. Adjust the seasoning with salt and pepper.

Cook the ziti in salted boiling water according to package directions. Strain the pasta and place it directly into the sugo (do not rinse with water). Top with the shaved cheese and Italian parsley.

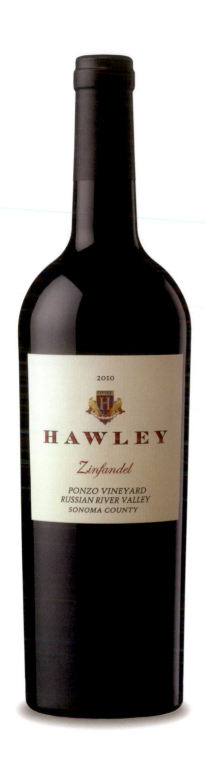

HAWLEY WINERY

Salsiccia (sahl-SEE-cy'yah) is Italian sausage, usually made from ground pork and seasoned with herbs and spices. At the market, it can be found either in casings, which are removed before cooking, or in bulk.

36 North Street
Healdsburg, CA 95448
707-473-9500
www.hawleywine.com

RIGATONI SALSICCIA

chef Craig Linowski, Baci Café & Wine Bar

Pair with Hawley Zinfandel

SERVES 6

1 pound fennel sausage,
   removed from casings
1 yellow onion, finely diced
1 tablespoon garlic, minced
3 ripe tomatoes
4 cups organic Italian tomato
   sauce
2 cups Hawley Zinfandel
salt and pepper to taste
½ cup Parmesan cheese,
   grated
1 pound dry rigatoni

In a large frying pan over medium heat, sauté the sausage until it's slightly brown. Drain off the grease, and add the onion, garlic and fresh tomatoes. Cook until the meat is coarse. Add the tomato sauce and wine, and let the mixture simmer for 1 hour. Add salt and pepper to taste.

Bring a large pot of salted water to a boil and add the pasta, cooking it until it's al dente, or firm to the bite. Toss the pasta with the salsiccia sauce, and when you're ready to serve, top with the grated cheese.

INSPIRATION VINEYARDS AND WINERY

This hearty pasta can be made any time of the year, as it calls for dried herbs in the seasonings. When they're in season, substitute with fresh marjoram, oregano, basil and tarragon.

3360 Coffey Lane, Suite E
Santa Rosa, CA 95401
707-237-4980
www.inspirationvineyards.com

ITALIAN SAUSAGE RAGU
with penne

chef Jon Phillips

Pair with Inspiration Vineyards Alexander Valley Zinfandel

SERVES 6

1 pound bulk ground Italian sausage (mild or spicy)

1 onion, minced

2 cloves garlic, pressed or finely minced

1/2 pound mushrooms, washed and sliced

1/2 cup Inspiration Vineyards Zinfandel

1 14.5-ounce can diced tomatoes

1 6-ounce can tomato paste

1/4 teaspoon marjoram

1/4 teaspoon oregano

1/4 teaspoon basil

1/4 teaspoon tarragon

1 pound penne pasta

Parmesan cheese, grated

In a large frying pan over medium-high heat, add the sausage, onion and garlic. Cook, stirring, until the sausage is cooked and the onion is opaque. Drain the grease from the pan, return the pan to the stovetop, and add the mushrooms. Continue cooking at medium heat until the moisture begins to evaporate from the mushrooms.

Add the wine, tomatoes, tomato paste and herbs. Reduce the heat to low and simmer the mixture for 1 hour. If it becomes too thick, add more wine in 1/4-cup increments to thin.

Prepare the pasta according to package directions and drain. Pour the meat ragu over the penne and mix to coat well. Serve with Parmesan cheese to taste.

MARTIN RAY WINERY

One of the best ways to create a successful wine and food match is to incorporate the wine that you'll serve into the dish. Our Angeline Russian River Valley Sauvignon Blanc is rich yet has a vibrant lemony zing; we use it in this recipe to tie in with the lemon juice and lemon zest in the risotto.

2191 Laguna Road
Santa Rosa, CA 95401
707-823-2404
www.martinraywinery.com

LEMON RISOTTO
with shrimp

chef Bruce Riezenman, Park Avenue Catering

Pair with Angeline Russian River Valley Sauvignon Blanc

SERVES 6

½ stick butter
¼ cup extra virgin olive oil
1 medium onion, finely
  minced
2 bay leaves
salt and pepper to taste
2 cups arborio rice
½ cup Russian River Valley
  Angeline Sauvignon Blanc
1 lemon, zest and juice
9 cups vegetable or chicken
  broth, hot
2 tablespoons Italian parsley,
  chopped
1 cup Parmesan cheese
¼ cup olive oil
1 pound shrimp, peeled and
  cleaned
1 teaspoon salt
pinch chili powder

Preheat oven to 400°.

In a saucepan over medium heat, place the butter and half of the olive oil. Add the onions, bay leaves, salt and pepper. Stir once and cover. Reduce the heat to low and cook for 8 to 10 minutes, until the onions are soft. Add the rice and stir until all the grains are coated. Add the wine and simmer until the liquid has been absorbed. Add the lemon zest.

Add half of the stock and stir. Simmer until the liquid is absorbed to just below rice level, stirring gently but frequently. Add most of the remaining broth 1 cup at a time (reserve 1 cup for later) until the rice has a very light "bite" to it, like al dente pasta.

When the rice is almost tender, stir in as much of the lemon juice as you'd like for a light lemony flavor. Gently stir in the last cup of broth, the parsley and the Parmesan. The risotto should be a little "soupy."

Toss the shrimp with the olive oil, salt and chili powder. Place the shrimp on a baking sheet and roast them in the oven for 5 to 7 minutes; remove them when just cooked. Serve on top of the risotto.

PAPAPIETRO PERRY
WINERY

This is comfort food at its best. Excellent quality ingredients will elevate this dish to something truly wonderful. You can add a combination of fresh and dried wild mushrooms to make it even more red-wine-friendly.

4791 Dry Creek Road
Healdsburg, CA 95448
707-433-0422
www.papapietro-perry.com

MAC & CHEESE
with bacon

chef Bruce Riezenman, Park Avenue Catering

Pair with Papapietro Perry Pinot Noir

SERVES 4

1 tablespoon butter
½ cup Japanese bread
   crumbs (panko)
1 tablespoon Italian parsley,
   chopped fine
10 bacon slices
1 tablespoon butter
3 tablespoons flour
½ cup chicken broth, cold (or
   vegetable broth)
2 cups milk, cold
2 teaspoons Dijon mustard
¾ pound elbow macaroni,
   cooked al dente
½ pound sharp white cheddar,
   grated
½ pound Monterey Jack,
   grated
1 ounce Vella Dry Jack, grated
kosher salt & freshly ground
   black pepper to taste

Preheat oven to 325°.

Add 1 tablespoon of butter and the bread crumbs to a sauté pan and cook until the mixture is golden. Season with salt and add the parsley. Set aside.

Bake the bacon in the preheated oven until it's crisp. Save the renderings. Blot the extra fat from the bacon and chop the slices into small pieces. Place 1 tablespoon of butter and 1 tablespoon of bacon renderings in a sauté pan over medium heat. When the butter starts to melt, add the flour. Mix, reduce the heat to low, and cook for 8 minutes, allowing only minimal browning.

Add the cold broth to the warm flour mixture a little at a time and stir until you get a smooth consistency. Place the pan over medium heat, and slowly add the milk in ½-cup increments, stirring until the mixture is smooth each time, and simmering before adding the next part. Once all the milk is added, add the mustard and let the mixture simmer for 30 minutes.

Combine the warm cream sauce, macaroni, cheeses and bacon. Add salt and pepper to taste. Place the mixture in a casserole and top it with the bread crumbs mixture. Bake for 20 minutes and serve hot.

SAPPHIRE HILL WINERY

Sharing great wine and food with friends is one of our biggest joys. The deep, rich fruit in our Winberrie Zinfandel makes it the perfect wine for drinking while you're preparing the dish, and also for enjoying with your guests. Add a fresh garden salad and some warm, crusty homemade bread to this recipe and you have a fabulous meal. The sauce is better if it's made a day ahead of time.

55 Front Street
Healdsburg, CA 95448
707-431-1888
www.sapphirehill.com

red pepper, spinach & goat cheese

RAVIOLI

with bison zinfandel marinara

chef Jeff Anderson

Pair with Sapphire Hill Winberrie Zinfandel

SERVES 6

SAUCE

3 tablespoons olive oil

1 pound ground bison

3 cloves garlic, diced

16 ounces crushed tomatoes

½ cup Sapphire Hill Zinfandel

½ cup water

1 teaspoon salt

1 teaspoon sugar

2 ounces fresh basil, chopped

RAVIOLI

1 pound basic pasta dough

6 ounces fresh goat cheese

4 ounces cream cheese

3 tablespoons fresh parsley, chopped

3 tablespoons fresh basil, chopped fine

1 teaspoon fresh thyme, chopped fine

6 ounces roasted red peppers, diced

4 ounces spinach leaves, chopped

salt and pepper to taste

3 ounces Parmesan cheese, grated

To prepare the sauce, heat the oil in a large skillet over medium heat. Add the bison and cook until almost brown. Add the garlic and continue to brown about 2 more minutes; be careful not to burn the garlic. Add the tomatoes, wine, water, salt and sugar. Cook over medium heat and bring to a boil. Reduce the heat to low and simmer about 30 minutes. Remove the skillet from the heat and stir in the chopped basil.

To make the ravioli, use a basic pasta dough recipe.

To make the filling, combine the goat cheese, cream cheese, parsley, 2 tablespoons of the basil, thyme, roasted red peppers and spinach, and season to taste with salt and pepper. Fill the ravioli and refrigerate them for at least 30 minutes.

Boil the ravioli until they're done. In a serving bowl, combine the ravioli with the sauce and toss to coat. Add the remaining basil and toss again.

To serve, divide the ravioli among 6 plates and top each with the Parmesan cheese.

SELBY WINERY

Inspired by a favorite dish of northern Italy, our arrabbiata sauce – that's "angry style" in Italian, referring to its spiciness – is a great combination with the classic, dry Piemonte wine called Dolcetto, which means "little sweet one." Betsy Covington, Ellen Brooks and Susie Selby created this recipe to match Susie's Russian River Valley Dolcetto. Serve it over your favorite pasta.

215 Center Street
Healdsburg, CA 95448
707-431-1703
www.selbywinery.com

SAUSAGE ARRABBIATA
& dolcetto

Pair with Selby Russian River Valley Dolcetto

SERVES 6

1 teaspoon olive oil

1 pound ground pork sausage, or cooked and quartered whole Italian sausage

1 cup onion, chopped

4 cloves garlic, minced

3/8 cup Selby Dolcetto

1 tablespoon sugar

1 tablespoon fresh basil, chopped

1 teaspoon crushed red pepper flakes

2 tablespoons tomato paste

1 tablespoon lemon juice

1/2 teaspoon Italian seasoning

1/4 teaspoon ground black pepper

2 14.5-ounce cans peeled and diced tomatoes

2 tablespoons fresh parsley, chopped

Heat the oil in a large saucepan over medium heat. Add the sausage and sauté it until it's lightly browned. Add the onion and garlic and sauté for 5 minutes.

Stir in the wine, sugar, basil, red pepper flakes, tomato paste, lemon juice, Italian seasoning, black pepper and tomatoes, and bring to a boil. Reduce the heat to medium, and simmer uncovered for approximately 15 minutes.

Stir in the parsley. Ladle the sauce over the hot cooked pasta of your choice.

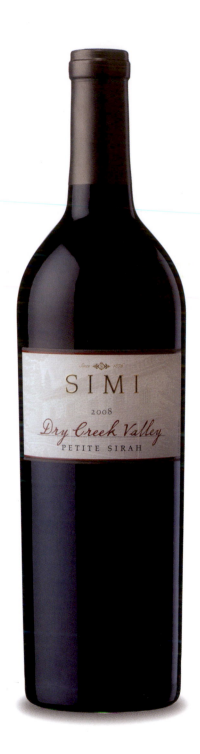

SIMI WINERY

Wild pigs roam the hillsides of western Sonoma County; if you're not a hunter, area butchers often have boar meat at their counters, so be sure to ask. This smoky, slightly rustic boar sauce is delicious served over any type of cooked pasta.

16275 Healdsburg Avenue
Healdsburg, CA 95448
707-433-6981
www.simiwinery.com

smoked
WILD BOAR BOLOGNESE

chef Eric Lee

Pair with Simi Dry Creek Valley Petite Sirah

SERVES 10

12 ounces wild boar shoulder or pork butt, cut into 1-1/2-inch cubes

1/4 cup extra virgin olive oil

2 ounces pancetta, finely diced

1-1/2 tablespoons garlic, minced

1 cup onion, finely diced

1/2 cup celery, finely diced

1/2 cup carrot, finely diced

1/2 cup milk

1 cup dry red wine

1 cup veal stock

1-1/2 cups diced tomatoes

1 tablespoon fresh thyme, chopped

1 tablespoon fresh oregano, chopped

2 tablespoons parsley, chopped

orange zest to taste

cinnamon to taste

salt and pepper to taste

Cold-smoke the boar at no more than 100° for about 30 minutes. Chill the meat for 2 hours and grind it through a coarse die.

In a frying pan, sauté the pancetta in the olive oil. Add the garlic, onion, celery and carrot and cook until tender. Add the ground meat and sauté the mixture until the boar is browned. Add the milk and reduce the mixture slightly. Then add the red wine and cook until the alcohol is evaporated, approximately 3 minutes.

Add the veal stock and tomatoes to the pan and let the sauce come to a boil. Continue to cook until the sauce is reduced by half. Add the herbs and season to taste with the orange zest, cinnamon, salt and pepper. Serve hot over cooked pasta.

THUMBPRINT CELLARS

As harvest comes to a close, grapes are fermenting their way to wine and thoughts of snow-covered Sierras and ski cabins begin to enter our minds. After long hours in the cellar, or on the slopes, we can't think of a better way to unwind than with a dish of Ryan's Pumpkin Gnocchi, a guest favorite from our wine and food pairings, enjoyed with a glass of our Zinfandel. Cheers to good food, good skiing and great Zin!

102 Matheson Street
Healdsburg, CA 95448
707-433-2393
www.thumbprintcellars.com

PUMPKIN GNOCCHI
with gorgonzola cream

vegi

chef Ryan Tunheim, Taste of Perfection Catering

Pair with Thumbprint Cellars Zinfandel

SERVES 8 TO 10

1 russet potato, cooked and
   mashed
½ cup canned pumpkin
2 egg yolks
½ teaspoon fresh nutmeg
3 cups flour
1 pint heavy cream
1 shallot, minced
8 ounces Gorgonzola cheese,
   crumbled
salt and freshly ground black
   pepper to taste
1 cup toasted pumpkin seeds

In a large bowl, combine the potato, pumpkin, egg yolks and nutmeg. Add the flour ½ cup at a time, mixing each time, until all the flour is incorporated.

Knead the dough until no visible flour is left, and divide the dough into quarters. Roll each quarter into long ropes, and cut into ½-inch pieces. Press each piece with the tines of a floured fork, and arrange the pieces on a floured sheet pan. Refrigerate for at least two hours.

In a saucepan, add the cream and shallot and bring the mixture to a boil over medium heat. Add the Gorgonzola and whisk (or use hand mixer) until the sauce is blended.

Bring a large pot of water to a boil over high heat, and add salt and the chilled gnocchi. Cook the gnocchi for 4 to 5 minutes, until they begin to float. Remove them from the water, allow them to drain well, and add them to the sauce. Stir to coat the gnocchi with the sauce, spoon them into individual serving bowls, and top with a sprinkling of toasted pumpkin seeds.

ENTRÉES

Lamb Shanks Braised in Chile Sauce
Sinfully Easy Lamb Kabobs
Boeuf Bourguignon
Sarah's Zinfandel Pork Sliders
Mexicali Beef Stew
Spiedini d'Agnello with Polenta di Bari
Duck Au "Zin"
Rimpinzarsi - Pig Out!
Hawaiian Kalua Pork with Rice
Grilled Tri-Tip with Bacon Chimichurri
Gerard's Paella
Cecil De Loach's Pulled Pork Sliders
Wild Salmon over Pinot Noir Risotto
Hungarian Goo-gau-lash
Cabernet-Marinated Steak
Pumpkin Risotto Cakes
Cabernet Braised Oxtail
Duck & Dumplings
California Chimichurri for Tri-Tip Steak
Willie Bird Turkey Gumbo
Beef Stroganoff
Short Ribs in Wine & Balsamic Sauce
Roasted Lavender Honey Duck Breast
Salsiccia con Pepperoni Sliders
Roasted Leg of Lamb with Aioli
Pulled Pork Sliders with Coleslaw

Mushroom-Braised Short Ribs
Smokin' Slow Moshin Brisket
Khoresht Fesenjaan (Chicken Stew)
Slow Roasted Pork Shoulder
Grilled Achiote Spiced Skirt Steak Tacos
Espresso-Braised Duck Sandwiches
Beef Brisket with Zinfandel Sauce
Manzo Brasato alla Lombarda
Smoked Lasagne di Melanzane
Grilled Duck Breast
Grilled Thai Curry Beef Skewers
Venison Stew with Robert Young Scion
Smoked Pork Tenderloin
Ratatouille with Lemon Pepper Polenta
Filet Mignon with Lobster Remoulade
Grilled Skirt Steak & Italian Fregola Salad
Charred Octopus with Arugula & Balsamic
Frane's Moussaka Lasagna
Pulled Pork Sandwiches with Slaw
Marmellata di Cipolle Rosse for Roast Pork
Polenta with Gorgonzola & Marinara Sauce
Mettie's Marvelous Meatballs
Pork with Panache
Inspire Burgers
Mushroom & Juniper Berry Short Ribs

ACORN WINERY/ ALEGRIA VINEYARDS

The creative inspiration for this dish was born out of Jeff and Susan Mall's work as restaurant consultants in Mexico. Lamb is a favorite meat of Acorn Winery owners Betsy & Bill Nachbaur, and they love Jeff Mall's use of spices with it.

12040 Old Redwood Highway
Healdsburg, CA 95448
707-433-6440
www.acornwinery.com

LAMB SHANKS

braised in cherry & guajillo chile sauce
with mashed acorn squash with rajas

chef Jeff Mall, Zin Restaurant & Wine Bar

Pair with Acorn Heritage Vines Zinfandel or Axiom Syrah

SERVES 6

LAMB

1 8-ounce bag dry guajillo chiles
6 lamb shanks
kosher salt and freshly ground
  black pepper
¼ cup olive oil
2 large yellow onions, diced
12 ounces frozen dark cherries,
  pitted
3 cloves garlic, peeled and sliced
1 tablespoon cumin seeds,
  toasted and ground
1 tablespoon plus 1 teaspoon
  Mexican oregano
1 bottle Zinfandel wine
1 quart chicken stock, unsalted
1 tablespoon kosher salt

SQUASH & RAJAS

2 pounds acorn or butternut
  squash, cut in half lengthwise,
  seeds removed
6 poblano peppers
2 tablespoons olive oil
2 yellow onions, sliced thin
2 tablespoons unsalted butter
½ cup heavy cream

Preheat oven to 350°.

Stem and remove the seeds from the chiles. Place them on a sheet pan and toast in the oven for 20 minutes. Place the toasted chiles in a bowl of hot water and let them rehydrate for 30 minutes. Drain well.

Season the lamb shanks with salt and pepper. Heat a 6- to 8-quart Dutch oven and add the olive oil. Heat the oil and carefully add the shanks. Brown them on all sides, remove them from the pan and set them aside.

Pour off all but 2 tablespoons of the oil. In the same Dutch oven, caramelize the onions until they're dark golden brown. Add the cherries, garlic, cumin and oregano. Add the Zinfandel, chicken stock and drained peppers. Bring to a boil, cover, and place in the oven. Cook 2 to 2-1/2 hours, or until the shanks are tender. Remove them from the pot, puree the remaining liquid, strain, and season to taste.

Place the squash, cut side down, on a sheet pan. Roast for 1 hour, or until the squash is totally soft to the touch. Set it aside to cool.

Toss the poblano peppers in the oil and char them on a grill until they're blackened. Let the peppers cool, then peel and cut them into strips (rajas). Heat a sauté pan, add the butter, and sauté the onions and peppers until they're well caramelized. Add the cream and reduce. Season to taste with salt. Scoop out the cooked squash flesh and fold into the poblanos. Season to taste with kosher salt and pepper.

To serve, slice the lamb and serve with the squash and rajas on the side.

ALEXANDER VALLEY VINEYARDS

This is our go-to recipe for entertaining when time is short. The dish is easy to make in advance, so all the work is done before guests arrive. It's also great to keep in the freezer for a quick weeknight meal – just serve with a Caesar salad. If you're not a lamb fan, substitute boneless chicken thighs in the recipe and serve Alexander Valley Vineyards Chardonnay instead of Sin Zin. If fresh herbs are not available, substitute with 2 teaspoons of dry herbes de provence.

8644 Highway 128
Healdsburg, CA 95448
707-433-7209
www.avvwine.com

sinfully easy
LAMB KABOBS

chef Pennie Haase

Pair with Alexander Valley Vineyards Sin Zin

SERVES 4-6

2 pounds boneless leg of
lamb

1-^{1}/$_2$ tablespoons garlic,
minced

1 tablespoon fresh rosemary,
minced

1 teaspoon fresh thyme
leaves, minced

1 tablespoon fresh Italian
parsley, minced

^{1}/$_4$ cup olive oil (preferably
from Alexander Valley
Vineyards)

^{1}/$_4$ cup Sin Zin

2 tablespoons red wine
vinegar

^{1}/$_2$ teaspoon Dijon mustard

^{1}/$_2$ teaspoon kosher salt

^{1}/$_2$ teaspoon black pepper,
coarsely ground

wood skewers

2 yellow onions, quartered

2 red bell peppers – cut into
1-^{1}/$_2$-inch pieces

Start this recipe 1 day ahead, trimming the lamb of excess fat and sinew. Cut it into 1-^{1}/$_2$-inch cubes.

In a large zip-lock plastic bag, add the garlic, herbs, olive oil, Zinfandel, red wine vinegar, mustard, salt and pepper, and mix well. Add the lamb cubes to the bag, seal tightly, and refrigerate overnight. You can also portion the lamb and marinade into serving sizes and freeze them for later use.

The next day, soak the skewers in water for 1 hour, so they don't catch fire during grilling.

Preheat a gas or charcoal grill to medium-hot.

Alternately thread the lamb, onion and red pepper onto skewers, and season with salt and pepper. Don't pack them together too tightly, as you want the heat to penetrate all surfaces. Grill the kabobs for 10 to 15 minutes, turning several times so that all sides brown evenly; the meat should be pink on the inside.

Serve with couscous and a mixed green salad.

BALLETTO VINEYARDS & WINERY

When the Praplan family opened La Gare restaurant in 1979, Roger cooked alongside his Swiss-born father, Marco Praplan, a renowned chef. Along with running the kitchen and cooking at La Gare, chef Roger also teaches courses at Santa Rosa Junior College on French cuisine, soups, stocks and classic sauces. La Gare's Beef Bourguignon recipe, handed-down from Marco to Roger, is the perfect dish for our luscious red wines. Marinate the lamb one day in advance.

5700 Occidental Road
Santa Rosa, CA 95401
707-568-2455
www.ballettovineyards.com

BOEUF BOURGUIGNON

chef Roger Praplan, Le Gare Restaurant

Pair with Balletto Pinot Noir

SERVES 6-8

MARINADE

3 pounds cubed beef, leg or outer round

1 onion, coarsely chopped

1 carrot, coarsely chopped

2 celery stalks, coarsely chopped

3 cloves garlic

1 bouquet garni (fresh sage, rosemary and thyme, tied up with kitchen string)

2 to 2-1/2 quarts Balletto Pinot Noir

BEEF BOURGUIGNON

salt and white pepper to taste

1/4 cup olive oil

2-3 ounces flour

3 cups demi-glace

6 ounces pearl onions

2 pounds button mushrooms, sautéed

6 ounces bacon, sautéed and diced

In a large container, combine all the marinade ingredients, cover, and refrigerate for at least 24 hours.

The next day, separate the meat from the vegetables, and the vegetables from the liquid. Remove the bouquet garni and reserve all.

Preheat oven to 375°.

Season the meat with salt and pepper. Heat the olive oil in a large Dutch oven and sear the meat cubes in the hot oil. Remove the meat and set it aside. Sauté the flour and the vegetables removed from the marinade, and place them in a stockpot. Deglaze the mixture with the marinade liquid.

Add the meat and bouquet garni, bring to a boil, and skim off the foam. Braise the beef in the oven for 1-1/2 to 2 hours.

When the meat is done, remove it from the liquid, reserving the liquid. Discard the bouquet garni. Strain the liquid, remove the fat, and add the demi-glace. Reduce to the desired consistency, adjust the seasoning with salt and pepper, and add the meat back to the sauce. Add the pearl onions, sautéed mushrooms and bacon. Serve hot.

CAROL SHELTON
WINES

Greg Hallihan made these sliders for our July 2010 celebration of the 10th anniversary of Carol Shelton Wines, and they were super popular with our "Carol's Bunch" wine club members and guests. They go with all of our Zins, but that day we toasted our 10 years of producing elegant Rockpile "Rocky Reserve" Zin and the wild-yeast-fermented Wild Thing Zin.

3354-B Coffey Lane
Santa Rosa CA 95403
707-575-3441
www.carolshelton.com

sarah's zinfandel
PORK SLIDERS

chef Greg Hallihan, Sarah's Forestville Kitchen

Pair with Carol Shelton Wild Thing Zinfandel

MAKES 60 SLIDERS

"THE RUB"

1-1/2 cups kosher salt

4 tablespoons smoked paprika
  (Penzeys.com has a nice version)

3 tablespoons cumin

1-1/2 tablespoons cayenne

1-1/2 tablespoons powdered garlic

1-1/2 tablespoons powdered onion

3 tablespoons dried ancho chile

SLIDERS

6-8 pounds pork shoulder or pork
  butt

32 ounces beef stock

1 bottle of Carol Shelton Wild Thing
  Zinfandel

2 bay leaves

1 whole onion, quartered

2 large carrots, chopped

2 ribs celery, chopped

60 dinner rolls or slider buns (or 16
  larger buns)

SLAW

1 cup mayonnaise

2 ounces cider vinegar

2 ounces honey

dash cayenne

1 head red cabbage, shredded

1 head green cabbage, shredded

2 carrots, shredded

In a small bowl, mix "The Rub" ingredients very well and massage the mixture evenly all over the pork.

Put the spice-rubbed pork in a large pot and add the beef stock, Zinfandel, bay leaves and chopped vegetables. Simmer on medium-low heat for 5 to 6 hours, covered, until the pork pulls apart easily.

Strain off the braising liquid and put it in the refrigerator for 2 hours. Skim off the fat cap that has formed at the top of the liquid and reduce the defatted liquid by about 1/3, over low heat.

Meanwhile, remove any fat and gristle from the pork, and using two forks, pull apart the meat into bite-sized pieces. You can do all of this ahead of time; reheat the pork prior to assembling the sliders.

To prepare the slaw, whisk together in a bowl the mayonnaise, vinegar, honey and cayenne. Toss the dressing with the shredded veggies just before use; if you do it too far ahead, it gets soggy.

To assemble the sliders, reheat the pork in the braising liquid reduction. Warm the rolls or buns on a grill or in the oven. Pile a big spoonful of pork on a bun bottom, cover with slaw, and add the top of the bun.

COLLIER FALLS
VINEYARDS

Barry Collier's vision for the Family Wineries Dry Creek Valley cooperative tasting room also goes for cooperative recipes, and this one is no exception. Chef Jeff Mall created this south-of-the-border version of beef stew to complement the fruit-forward, spicy, classic Zinfandel Barry produces from one of the northernmost hillsides in Dry Creek Valley.

4791 Dry Creek Road
Healdsburg, CA 95448
707-433-0100
www.familywines.com

MEXICALI BEEF STEW

chef Jeff Mall, Zin Restaurant & Wine Bar

Pair with Collier Falls Private Reserve Dry Creek Valley Zinfandel

SERVES 6

6 dry New Mexico chile peppers

6 dry California chile peppers

6 dry pasilla chile peppers

2 pounds boneless beef chuck roast

2 ounces bacon

6 cloves garlic, sliced

2 yellow onions, small dice

1-1/2 teaspoons whole cumin seeds, toasted and ground

3 cups tomato puree

1 cup Zinfandel

1-1/2 cups chicken stock

2 cups butternut squash, 1/2-inch dice

1 cup cooked hominy

salt to taste

Preheat oven to 400°.

Using kitchen shears, cut the peppers into small pieces, removing the seeds and stems as you go. (You may want to wear rubber gloves while doing this.) Place the peppers on a cookie sheet and toast them in the oven for 10 minutes. Place the peppers in a blender with 1 cup of warm water, and puree to a thick paste.

Cut the chuck roast into 1-inch-square cubes, removing any excess fat, and dice the bacon into small pieces. In a large, heavy duty stockpot, render the bacon over medium heat, add the diced chuck, and brown the meat on all sides. Add the garlic and onions, and cook until they're golden brown.

Add the ground cumin, tomato puree, Zinfandel, stock and the pureed chile peppers, and bring the mixture to a boil. Reduce the heat to a slow simmer, and cook the stew, uncovered, for 2 hours, or until the meat is tender.

Add the squash and hominy, and cook for 30 minutes more, or until the squash is tender. Season to taste with salt, and serve, accompanied with cheddar and green onion corn muffins.

D'ARGENZIO WINERY

This is an old family immigrant recipe traditionally served on Sunday afternoons. Spiedini d'agnello are skewers of lamb and vegetables, and we like to serve them with polenta di Bari, named for the southeastern Italy coastal town of Bari, where polenta and lamb are staples. Marinate the lamb one day ahead of time.

1301 Cleveland Avenue
Santa Rosa, CA 95401
707-280-4658
www.dargenziowine.com

SPIEDINI D'AGNELLO
with polenta di bari

chef Rosa d'Loiodice

Pair with D'Argenzio Russian River Valley Zinfandel

SERVES 4

LAMB

1 pound boneless leg of lamb, trimmed and cut into 1-inch cubes
2 tablespoons extra virgin olive oil
sea salt
black pepper
2 tablespoons wine vinegar
1 tablespoon fresh Italian parsley, chopped
1 tablespoon fresh mint, chopped
1 tablespoon fresh fennel, chopped
kabob skewers
1 yellow bell pepper, cut into 1-inch chunks
1 red bell pepper, cut into 1-inch chunks
1 large yellow onion, cut into 1-inch chunks

POLENTA

1 cup water
2 cups white wine
1 cup coarse-ground polenta
3 tablespoons unsalted butter
1-$\frac{1}{2}$ teaspoons sea salt
$\frac{1}{4}$ teaspoon freshly ground black pepper
2 ounces Parmesan, grated

In a large bowl, add the cubed lamb, oil, salt, pepper, vinegar, parsley, mint and fennel, and mix well. Cover the bowl and let the lamb mixture marinate overnight in the refrigerator.

The next day, remove the lamb from the marinade. On each skewer, thread, in order, two lamb cubes, 1 pepper chunk, 1 onion chunk and two more lamb cubes.

Grill the skewers for 6 to 8 minutes, until the lamb is cooked to the desired doneness. Transfer the spiedini to a warm plate for 5 minutes before serving.

To prepare the polenta, in a large pot, boil the water and wine for 10 minutes. Add the polenta, bring the mixture to a simmer, cover the pot and cook for 35 to 40 minutes, stirring every 10 minutes. Add the butter, salt and pepper, stir, and then gradually add the Parmesan.

Serve the hot polenta with the lamb skewers.

DASHE CELLARS

Here is a classic pairing of Zinfandel and duck – and of master craftsmen, Dashe winemaker Mike Dashe and chef Jeff Mall.

4791 Dry Creek Road
Healdsburg, CA 95448
707-433-0100 x1
www.familywines.com

DUCK AU "ZIN"

chef Jeff Mall, Zin Restaurant & Wine Bar

Pair with Dashe Florence Vineyard Dry Creek Valley Zinfandel

SERVES 6

6 whole duck legs

kosher salt

freshly ground black pepper

1 teaspoon fresh thyme,
   minced

¼ cup olive oil

6 slices applewood-smoked
   bacon, diced

3 cloves garlic, sliced thin

2 shallots, minced

¼ pound crimini mushrooms,
   cleaned and stems removed

½ pound boiling onions,
   peeled of their paper skin

1 bottle Dashe Zinfandel

2 cups dark chicken stock

2 bay leaves

Season the duck legs with salt, pepper and thyme, and set aside.

Heat a Dutch oven over medium heat. Add the olive oil, then the bacon, and cook the bacon until it's crisp. Remove the bacon to paper towels to drain.

In the same Dutch oven, brown the seasoned duck legs in the bacon fat/oil, skin side down, until they're well browned. Remove the duck legs from the pan and set them aside.

Sauté the garlic and shallots in the fat left in the pot, until they're translucent. Add the mushrooms and boiling onions, and cook until the mushrooms release most of their liquid. Return the bacon and duck to the pot.

Deglaze the pot with the wine. Add the stock and bring the mixture to a boil. Add the bay leaves, and reduce to a simmer.

Cook the duck, covered, over low heat for 2 hours, or until the meat is tender. Skim the fat from the top of the sauce and adjust the seasoning, if necessary.

Serve the duck with mashed root vegetables, and garnish with chives.

DAVIS FAMILY VINEYARDS

This creation comes to us from John Stewart and Duskie Estes of Zazu Restaurant and Farm, Bovolo restaurant and Black Pig Meat Company. Our son, Cooper Davis, worked with the Zazu team on the dish and will present it at "A Wine & Food Affair." It gets its deep flavor from the slow cooking of the pork, yet the secret is in browning the onions and garlic in olive oil – which the Italians call soffritto.

52 Front Street
Healdsburg, CA 95448
707-433-3858
www.davisfamilyvineyards.com

RIMPINZARSI

(italian for "pig out")

chefs John Stewart & Duskie Estes, Zazu Restaurant and Farm

Pair with Davis Family Soul Patch Pinot Noir

SERVES 6

3 pounds pork shoulder, cut into 1-inch cubes

¼ cup flour

¼ cup olive oil, divided

1 medium red onion, chopped

1 tablespoon garlic, chopped

½ cup chicken stock

2-½ cups Davis Family Pinot Noir

1 bay leaf

1 14-ounce can whole tomatoes, roughly chopped

2 carrots, medium dice

2 cups canned white beans

In small batches, toss the pork cubes in a bowl with the flour. Heat ½ of the measured oil in a sauté pan, add the floured pork, and cook until the meat is browned. Remove the pork from the pan and place it on paper towels to dry.

Discard the oil from the pan, wipe it clean, and add the remaining fresh oil. Heat the oil, add the onions and garlic, and cook until they're browned. Return the pork to the pan, add the chicken stock, wine and bay leaf, and simmer slowly for approximately 3 hours, until the meat is tender.

Add the tomatoes, carrots and beans, and simmer for 30 minutes more. Season to taste with salt and pepper, and serve with a loaf of toasted, crusty bread.

DELOACH VINEYARDS

This is the most traditional of all Hawaiian luau dishes. We were inspired by and taught to prepare it by our absolute favorite Hawaiian chef, Allen C. Hess, who was raised in Sonoma County and is the son of DeLoach sous chef Lisa Porter. We'll serve the pork with Allen's garlic and macadamia nut rice, but if we gave you that recipe, we'd have to kill you. Aloha!

1791 Olivet Road
Santa Rosa, CA 95401
707-526-9111
www.deloachvineyards.com

HAWAIIAN KALUA PORK
with rice

chefs Sue Boy & Lisa Porter

Pair with DeLoach Russian River Valley Pinot Noir

SERVES 4

6 ti or 2 banana leaves (found in Asian markets)

6 pounds pork butt, cut into 6 pieces about 2 inches thick

2-1/2 tablespoons Hawaiian (preferred) or kosher salt

2-1/2 tablespoons all-natural liquid smoke flavoring (no chemicals or preservatives)

Preheat oven to 500°.

Place a piece of aluminum foil measuring 9 inches by 11 inches on a flat work surface. Place 3 ti leaves or 1 banana leaf on top of the foil, and the pork pieces on top of the leaves. Sprinkle the meat with the salt and liquid smoke. Place the remaining 3 ti leaves or banana leaf on top of the pork. Cover with additional foil and seal tightly.

Place the package in a large roasting pan, fill it with 2 inches of water, and cover the pan with foil to seal in the steam. Cook for 1-1/2 to 2 hours, or until the pork is tender. When it's cool, shred the pork, and serve it with steamed white rice or your favorite rice dish.

deLORIMIER WINERY

You can never go wrong with bacon! I loved combining some of my favorite ingredients to create this wonderful recipe. The higher quality of wine you use in the dish, the better the results.

2001 Highway 128
Geyserville, CA 95441
707-857-2000
www.delorimierwinery.com

GRILLED TRI-TIP
with bacon chimichurri

chef Ryan Waldron

Pair with deLorimier Crazy Creek Vineyard Alexander Valley Cabernet Sauvignon

SERVES 4-6

MEAT

1 cup Cabernet Sauvignon
2 tablespoons extra virgin
   olive oil
6 garlic cloves, minced
1 medium red onion, minced
3 tablespoons thyme
3 tablespoons rosemary
salt and pepper to taste
1 large tri-tip steak

CHIMICHURRI

4 garlic cloves
1/2 cup flat leaf parsley,
   packed
1/4 cup oregano leaves,
   packed
juice of 1 small lemon
1/4 cup rice vinegar
1 cup extra virgin olive oil
salt and pepper to taste
8 slices thick-cut bacon

First marinate the tri-tip. Combine all the ingredients except for the meat in a zip-lock bag, then add the tri-tip. Squeeze out all the air. Refrigerate for 4 hours, or overnight.

To prepare the chimichurri sauce, using as food processor or stick blender, combine the garlic, parsley, oregano, lemon juice, vinegar and olive oil. Process them until the ingredients are well pureed. Season lightly with salt and pepper. Cook the bacon until it's crisp. Save 2 tablespoons of the bacon fat, and chop the bacon when it's cooled.

Remove the tri-tip from the marinade and grill it to the desired temperature – about 120° for medium-rare. Let the meat rest for 5 minutes after removing it from the grill.

Heat the bacon fat in a saucepan, add the chimichurri sauce, and bring the mixture to a simmer. Remove the pan from the heat and add the bacon.

Slice the tri-tip 1/2-inch thick, against the grain. To serve, fan the slices on a plate and add the sauce; sautéed Swiss chard and fingerling potatoes are fine accompaniments.

GRATON RIDGE CELLARS

Feel free to substitute piquillo peppers for the red bell peppers; slender asparagus pieces or baby artichoke hearts for the green beans; and New Zealand mussels for the Manila clams.

3561 Gravenstein Highway North
Sebastopol, CA 95472
707-823-3040
www.gratonridge.com

gerard's
PAELLA

chef Gerard Nebesky

Pair with Graton Ridge Cellars Russian River Valley Pinot Noir

SERVES 10

1 cup olive oil

2 to 3 heads garlic, cloves detached but not peeled

6 red peppers, cored, seeded and sliced

5 to 6 pounds chicken legs and thighs, bone in

4 yellow onions, chopped

2 16-ounce cans diced tomatoes

6 to 7-1/2 cups chicken stock

20 to 25 saffron threads, crushed

2 to 2-1/2 teaspoons smoked Spanish paprika

4 to 5 cups short-grain rice, uncooked

2 16-ounce cans garbanzo beans

1 pound green beans

20 to 24 jumbo shrimp, 16/20 count

20 to 24 Manila clams

4 to 5 lemons, cut into wedges

Heat a paella pan (or a large, flat-bottomed sauté pan) over medium-high heat. Add the olive oil and garlic, heat through, add the peppers and fry them until they're tender. Remove the peppers and set them aside. Add the chicken pieces to the pan, searing them on all sides. When the chicken is golden, add the onions and sauté until they're translucent. Add the tomatoes and the stock, and reduce the base down for about 30 minutes.

Meanwhile, crush the saffron with the smoked paprika in a mortar and add it to the stock. After 30 minutes, stir in the rice and let it simmer for about 20 minutes. Important: Do not stir or cover the rice. As it cooks, add the vegetables and the green beans and garbanzo beans.

During the final 10 minutes, poke the shrimp and clams into the rice mixture so that they will cook. You will know the dish is done when you can smell the smoky odor of the rice caramelizing on the bottom of the pan, and all the liquid is absorbed by the rice.

Finish the dish with a squeeze of lemon, and leave the lemon wedges in the pan or perched along the rim.

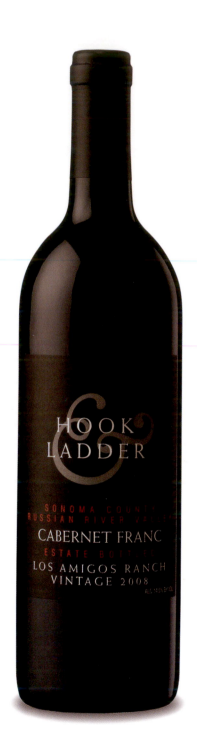

HOOK & LADDER
WINERY

When I was a boy growing up in Macon, Georgia, our family's favorite barbecue was a place called Fincher's. This pulled pork sandwich is my humble attempt to produce that Fincher's sandwich from my childhood. I like to serve the sandwich with vegetarian Southwest beans, coleslaw and a kosher-style dill pickle.

2134 Olivet Road
Santa Rosa, CA 95401
707-526-2255
www.hookandladderwinery.com

cecil de loach's
PULLED PORK SLIDERS

Pair with Hook & Ladder Russian River Valley Cabernet Franc

MAKES 30 SLIDERS

5-pound pork butt, cut into
  1-1/2-inch cubes
3/4 cup apple cider vinegar
1 cup water
1 tablespoon kosher salt
1/2 teaspoon black pepper
1 teaspoon crushed red
  pepper flakes
1 teaspoon granulated garlic
1 teaspoon Colman's Dry
  Mustard
1 teaspoon ground white
  pepper
3/4 cup ketchup
Tabasco sauce, to taste
1 to 2 teaspoons molasses, to
  taste
1/2 teaspoon Wright's Hickory
  Seasoning Liquid Smoke
30 mini hamburger buns

Place the meat on the rack of a pressure cooker. In a bowl, mix the next 9 ingredients (through ketchup) together and stir the mixture into the meat.

Turn on the heat in the pressure cooker and cook the pork according to the directions for your equipment at level 2, or the higher cooking method, for 30 minutes. Remove the cooker from the heat and let the pressure reduce on its own. Once the pressure is reduced, open the pressure cooker, pull the meat apart with 2 forks, and mix in the Tabasco, molasses and liquid smoke.

Return the cooker to the heat, without the lid, and reduce the liquid as needed.

To serve, stir to blend all the ingredients, and pile the pork and sauce onto mini hamburger buns.

HOP KILN WINERY

This traditional Italian pairing of fish and risotto is simple and elegant. The rich, flavorful wild salmon and earthy mushrooms complement the flavors of HKG Pinot Noir. Chef Renzo Veronese calls it "Salmone con Risotto di Vino Rosso e Funghi;" you'll call it simply delicious.

6050 Westside Road
Healdsburg, CA 95448
707-433-6491
www.hopkilnwinery.com

WILD SALMON

with crimini mushrooms over pinot noir risotto

chef Renzo Veronese

Pair with Hop Kiln HKG Russian River Valley Pinot Noir

SERVES 4

RISOTTO

2 tablespoons extra virgin olive oil

¼ cup white onion, finely diced

1-½ cups arborio rice

7 cups chicken stock

1-½ cups HKG Pinot Noir

4 tablespoons unsalted butter

¼ cup Parmigiano Reggiano cheese, grated

salt and pepper to taste

SALMON

4 6-ounce wild salmon filets

salt and pepper to taste

3 teaspoons extra virgin olive oil

2 cups crimini mushrooms, sliced

1 clove garlic, minced

½ cup HKG Pinot Noir

2 tablespoons unsalted butter

2 tablespoons Italian parsley, chopped

To prepare the risotto, in a 10-inch sauté pan, heat the olive oil over medium heat.

Add the onions and cook them until they're softened. Then add the rice and stir with a wooden spoon for 2-3 minutes.

Slowly add 2 cups of the chicken stock, stirring until the liquid is fully absorbed. Add the Pinot Noir, stirring until the wine is fully absorbed by rice. Slowly stir in the remaining chicken stock, stopping when the rice is plump and tender, and all liquid has been absorbed. Stir in the butter and cheese, mix well and season with salt and pepper.

To prepare the salmon, preheat the oven to 500°. Season the fish with salt and pepper. In a hot skillet with 1 teaspoon of olive oil, brown the salmon on each side for about 1 minute. Cook the salmon in the oven for about 5 minutes, until the fish is just cooked in the center.

Meanwhile, prepare the mushrooms by heating the remaining 2 teaspoons of olive oil in a sauté pan over medium heat. Add the mushrooms and garlic and sauté until they're browned and soft. Stir in the wine and butter and let the mixture reduce.

Finish with 1 teaspoon of parsley.

To serve, place the risotto on the center of the plate, and carefully lay the salmon on the rice. Spoon on the mushrooms, and finish with a sprinkling of the remaining parsley.

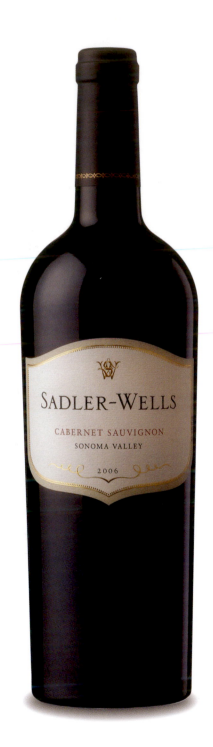

HUDSON STREET WINERIES

Bill Spear of Sadler-Wells Wines first made this dish about 15 years ago, when our children were still quite young. Everybody just loved it! When we asked one of our girls what she wanted for her birthday dinner, she said "Goo-gau-lash," and we've said it that way ever since. You can freeze any leftovers; serve them over fresh-cooked noodles for a quick and delicious meal later.

428 Hudson Street
Healdsburg, CA 95448
707-433-2364
www.hudsonstreeetwineries.com

hungarian
GOO-GAU-LASH

chef Bill Spear

Pair with Sadler-Wells Cabernet Sauvignon

SERVES 12

¼ cup unsalted butter

¼ cup olive oil

5 pounds beef chuck, well-trimmed and cut into 1-inch cubes

salt and freshly ground black pepper

5 pounds yellow onions, chopped

2 pounds red bell pepper, chopped

½ cup Hungarian paprika

3 cups beef stock

2 pounds broad egg noodles, cooked

sour cream, for garnish

chives, chopped, for garnish

Heat 1 tablespoon of the butter and 1 tablespoon of the olive oil in a large, heavy-bottomed pot over high heat. Season the meat with salt and pepper to taste. Cook the meat in batches, adding 1 tablespoon each of butter and oil as needed. Cook each batch until the meat is browned on all sides, about 3 to 5 minutes. Transfer the meat and juices to a plate with each batch.

Reduce the heat to low, add the onions, and cook, stirring occasionally, until the onions are translucent, about 15 to 20 minutes. Add the red bell pepper and stir for about 2 minutes. Return the meat and juices to the pot, and add the paprika and stock. Stir well to combine.

Cook the mixture, covered, over very low heat, stirring occasionally, until the meat is tender and the sauce has thickened, about 1-1/2 to 2 hours. Adjust the seasoning, if necessary.

To serve, ladle the "Goo-gau-lash" over the cooked egg noodles and top with a dollop of sour cream and a sprinkling of chives.

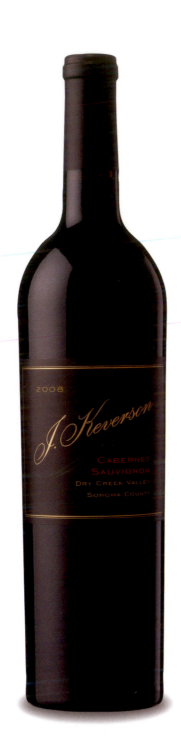

J. KEVERSON WINERY

One fall day, we had one of our bocce games, which always included dinner and wine, but an unexpected rain ended our game. Instead of throwing the tri-tip on the barbecue, we decided to roast it in the oven. Everyone loved the way it turned out, and now it's our preferred method for cooking on those rainy days and cold evenings when we want to serve something hearty and comforting. Marinate the meat one night in advance.

53 Front Street
Healdsburg, CA 95448
707-433-3097
www.jkeverson.com

cabernet-marinated
STEAK WITH BLUE CHEESE

chef Diane Bard

Pair with J. Keverson Cabernet Sauvignon

SERVES 4

MARINADE

1 cup J. Keverson Cabernet
   Sauvignon

1/4 cup olive oil

3 tablespoons balsamic vinegar

1/4 cup Mission figs, diced

1/2 red onion, chopped

2 shallots, diced

2 garlic cloves, sliced

1 sprig fresh thyme

sea salt and freshly ground pepper

1 pound tri-tip steak

DRESSING

1 shallot, chopped

4 tablespoons blue cheese

1/2 cup sour cream

1/4 cup cream cheese, softened

freshly ground black pepper

REDUCTION

2 cups J. Keverson Cabernet
   Sauvignon

1/4 cup balsamic vinegar

1 shallot, diced

2 Mission figs, diced

1 teaspoon peppercorns

2 teaspoons honey

salt

To prepare the meat, put all the marinade ingredients in a large zip-lock plastic bag. Shake the bag to blend the ingredients and coat the meat, and put it in the refrigerator overnight.

The next day, preheat the oven to 375°.

Transfer the meat and marinade to a baking dish. Season the steak with more salt and pepper, cover the dish tightly with foil, and roast the tri-tip in the oven until it's done (an internal temperature of 135°-145° is medium to medium-rare). Remove the thyme sprig and discard.

While the meat roasts, prepare the blue cheese dressing by adding all the ingredients to a food processor and pulsing they're until well blended. Check for seasoning, and set aside.

When the tri-tip is done, remove it from the oven and let it rest for 10 minutes. During this time, prepare the reduction sauce by combining the wine, vinegar, shallot, figs and peppercorns in a medium saucepan over high heat. Bring the mixture to a boil, then lower the heat to medium-low and cook until the sauce thickens by about half. Pour the sauce through a strainer into a bowl and discard the solids. Add the honey, and season to taste with salt.

To serve, slice the rested steak across the grain. Place the steak slices on a platter and pour the cooking juices over all. Drizzle the meat with the reduction sauce and top with a dollop of blue cheese dressing.

KACHINA VINEYARDS

In love with pumpkin and goat cheese, I created this dish to salute the flavors of fall. These risotto cakes are savory and comforting, and the Cabernet Sauvignon reduction sauce ties the dish to the wine.

4551 Dry Creek Road
Healdsburg, CA 95448
707-332-7917
www.kachinavineyards.com

PUMPKIN RISOTTO CAKES
with goat cheese & balsamic cabernet reduction

vegi

chef Mike Matson, Vintage Valley Catering

Pair with Kachina Dry Creek Valley Cabernet Sauvignon

SERVES 8

RISOTTO CAKES

2 tablespoons peanut oil

1 cup shallots, sliced

1 tablespoon garlic, chopped

2 cups arborio rice

5 cups vegetable stock, heated

2 cups roasted and pureed spiced pumpkin

3/4 cup Parmesan cheese, grated

1 cup fresh goat cheese

2 tablespoons fresh sage, chopped

3 tablespoons butter

CABERNET REDUCTION

1 tablespoon olive oil

1 medium shallot, minced

1/4 teaspoon salt

1/2 teaspoon freshly ground pepper

1 cup Kachina Cabernet Sauvignon

1/4 cup balsamic vinegar

2 tablespoons honey

4 sprigs fresh thyme

2 tablespoons butter

To prepare the risotto cakes, in a large sauté pan, heat the peanut oil and add the shallots and garlic. Cook until the shallots are translucent.

Add the rice to the pan, stir, and gradually add the heated vegetable stock. Cook, stirring continuously, until the rice is slightly softer than al dente. Add the pumpkin, Parmesan, goat cheese, sage and 2 tablespoons of the butter, and stir to combine. Spread the mixture on a sheet pan to cool.

When the risotto mixture has cooled, cut it into the desired shape (squares, rounds, diamonds, etc.). In a sauté pan, add the remaining 1 tablespoon of butter and cook the cakes on each side for 1-1/2 minutes.

Meanwhile, prepare the Cabernet reduction sauce. Heat the olive oil in a small saucepan over medium-high heat. Add the shallot and cook until it's soft but not brown. Season with salt and pepper.

Add the wine, vinegar, honey and thyme, and whisk to combine. Increase the heat to high and bring the mixture to a boil. Then reduce the heat to medium-high and boil the sauce until it's reduced by half. Strain the sauce into a small bowl, and return the strained liquid to the pan, warming over low heat. Whisk in the butter until it's melted, and adjust the seasoning if necessary.

Serve the cakes with mixed greens drizzled with the Cabernet reduction.

KENDALL-JACKSON WINE CENTER

Oxtail is braised low and slow in our Cabernet Sauvignon until it falls off the bone and creates a lush, velvety sauce. Stone-ground grits from the Old Mill of Guilford in North Carolina make for a soulfully smooth pairing with our high-elevation Cabernet.

5007 Fulton Road
Fulton, CA 95439
707-571-8100
www.kj.com

CABERNET-BRAISED OXTAIL
with heirloom tomato & okra sauce

chef Justin Wangler

Pair with Kendall-Jackson Jackson Hills Cabernet Sauvignon

SERVES 8

OXTAIL
1 quart veal stock
2 quarts water
8 pounds oxtail
kosher salt
1/4 cup rice oil
1 large onion, large dice
2 medium carrots, large dice
4 stalks celery, large dice
2 tablespoons tomato paste
1 cup Cabernet Sauvignon
4 sprigs fresh thyme
2 bay leaves
4 parsley stems

GRITS
2-1/2 cups water
1/2 cup milk
1/2 cup grits
kosher salt
1/2 cup cream
1 tablespoon butter

SAUCE
1 small onion, small dice
2 stalks celery, small dice
2 medium carrots, small dice
1/4 cup vegetable oil
1 cup Cabernet Sauvignon, reduced by half
2 cups roasted heirloom tomato sauce
1 cup okra, sliced
1 tablespoon fresh thyme, chopped
kosher salt
1/4 cup fresh parsley, chopped

To prepare the oxtail, preheat the oven to 300°.

In a large pot, bring the veal stock and water to a boil.

Season the oxtail with salt. In a heavy-bottomed sauté pan, brown the oxtail in the rice oil over high heat. Transfer the meat to a braising pan.

Remove the excess fat from the sauté pan and add the onions, carrots and celery. Cook until they're caramelized, then add the tomato paste. Stir and continue to cook to caramelize again. Add the wine, and with a wooden spoon, scrape up the bits from the bottom of the pan.

Transfer the contents of the sauté pan to the braising pan and add the hot veal/water mixture. Add the thyme, bay leaves and parsley, cover with foil, and roast in the oven for 2-1/2 hours, or until the oxtail is tender. Let it cool in the pan liquid for 1 hour.

Remove the oxtail from the braising pan and discard the bones, fat and gristle. Strain the cooking liquid and skim off the fat. In a saucepan over medium heat, reduce the liquid by half, and reserve.

Next, prepare the grits. In a large pot, add the water and milk, and bring to a boil. Slowly add the grits and whisk vigorously until the mixture thickens. Simmer for 45 minutes, then whisk in the cream and butter.

While the grits cook, prepare the tomato-okra sauce. In a large pot, sweat the diced vegetables in oil over low heat, until they're tender. Do not caramelize! Add the oxtail, reduced Cabernet Sauvignon, reduced cooking liquid, tomato sauce, okra and thyme. Bring the mixture to a simmer and season with salt.

To serve, ladle a portion of grits into each bowl and top with the oxtail sauce. Garnish with the chopped parsley.

KOKOMO WINERY

This is a new twist on an old dish. It's chicken and dumplings, wine country style, and it's sure to excite Pinot Noir lovers – California fusion at its best. Peace, love and Pinot!

4791 Dry Creek Road
Healdsburg, CA 95448
707-433-0200
www.kokomowines.com

DUCK & DUMPLINGS

chefs Jason Denton & Josh Silvers, Jackson's Bar and Oven

Pair with Kokomo Winemaker's Reserve Peters Vineyard Sonoma Coast Pinot Noir

SERVES 6-8

DUMPLINGS
2 cups all-purpose flour
2 teaspoons baking powder
3/4 teaspoon salt
1/4 cup minced fresh herb
  leaves (parsley, chives and/or
  tarragon)
2 tablespoons duck fat
3/4 cup milk

DUCK
6 tablespoons duck fat
6 tablespoons all-purpose flour
2 tablespoons dry sherry
6 cups duck stock (or chicken
  stock)
1 large onion, diced
3 celery stalks, diced
4 medium carrots, peeled and
  diced
2 bay leaves
2 cups duck leg meat, diced
1 tablespoon heavy cream
1 teaspoon fresh thyme
salt and black pepper to taste
3/4 cup frozen peas, thawed
1/4 cup parsley, minced

To prepare the dumpling dough, sift together the flour, baking powder and salt in a medium bowl. Add the herbs and combine, then add the duck fat and milk. Gently mix with a spoon until the mixture just comes together; do not overmix, or the dumplings will be too dense. Set aside.

To prepare the duck, heat the duck fat in a pan. Whisk in the flour and cook, whisking constantly, until the flour turns golden, 1 to 2 minutes. Whisking constantly, gradually add the sherry, then slowly add the duck stock. Simmer until the mixture thickens slightly, 2 to 3 minutes.

Stir in the onion, celery, carrots and bay leaves, and simmer for 5 minutes. Stir in the duck meat, cream and thyme, and return to a simmer. Add the salt and black pepper to taste.

Drop the dumpling batter into the simmering duck stew by heaping teaspoonfuls. Cover the pan and simmer until the dumplings are cooked through, about 15 minutes. Once you have covered the pan, do not uncover it while the dumplings are cooking. In order for them to be light and fluffy, they must steam, not boil. Uncovering the pan releases the steam.

Gently stir in the peas and parsley, and serve.

KRUTZ FAMILY CELLARS

Grill a tri-tip steak, top it with this special California Chimichurri, and pour a glass of Syrah for a real Cal-Argentine experience. Salud!

1301 Cleveland Avenue, Suite B
Santa Rosa, CA 95401
707-536-1532
www.krutzfamilycellars.com

CALIFORNIA CHIMICHURRI

for grilled tri-tip steak

Pair with Krutz Family Cellars Syrah

1 cup fresh Thai basil, packed
¼ cup fresh cilantro, packed
½ cup olive oil
⅓ cup red wine vinegar
2 garlic cloves, peeled
¾ teaspoon fresh Thai chile, minced
½ teaspoon ground cumin
½ teaspoon salt
¼ teaspoon ground star anise

Grill a tri-tip steak to your preferred doneness. Let it rest for 10 minutes.

Meanwhile, place all the chimichurri ingredients in a blender or food processor, and blend well.

Slice the tri-tip and pour the sauce over the slices. Alternatively, serve the steak with the chimichurri in dipping bowls.

LA CREMA TASTING ROOM

This gumbo will develop more flavor the longer it's cooked. Be sure to stir and cook it slowly, over very low heat. Serve over white rice.

235 Healdsburg Avenue
Healdsburg, CA 95448
707-431-9400
www.lacrema.com

willie bird
TURKEY GUMBO

chef Andrei Litvinenko

Pair with La Crema Sonoma County Syrah

SERVES 8

1 cup vegetable oil

2 cups flour

2 cups onion, diced

1 cup celery, diced

1 cup green bell peppers, diced

4 cloves garlic, minced

1 pound andouille sausage, diced

4 boneless turkey thighs, diced

1 12-ounce can diced tomatoes

4 quarts chicken stock

1 tablespoon Worcestershire sauce

1 tablespoon Tabasco sauce

1 tablespoon paprika

1 tablespoon garlic powder

1 tablespoon onion powder

1 tablespoon oregano

½ teaspoon cayenne pepper

½ teaspoon celery seed

1 teaspoon freshly ground black pepper

2 tablespoons filé powder

2 cups okra, sliced

kosher salt to tast

In a large, heavy-bottomed pot, heat the oil over medium-low heat. Add the flour and continue to stir, until the roux turns very dark brown (this may take up to 30 minutes).

Add the onion, celery, bell peppers and garlic, and cook for 10 minutes. Add the sausage and turkey, and cook for 5 minutes. Add the tomatoes, chicken stock, Worcestershire, Tabasco, paprika, garlic powder, oregano, cayenne, celery seed and pepper, and stir to combine.

Cook until the mixture thickens for at least 1 hour. Add the filé powder and okra, mix, and cook for 10 minutes. Add salt to taste, and serve over rice.

LA CREMA WINERY

This is a classic and sometimes under-appreciated dish, which takes on supreme status when it's paired with Pinot Noir. Serve it over egg noodles, rice or mashed potatoes.

3690 Laughlin Road
Windsor, CA 95492
707-571-1504
www.lacrema.com

BEEF STROGANOFF

Pair with La Crema Russian River Valley Pinot Noir

SERVES 8

¼ cup butter

2 pounds beef top round, sliced into thin strips

2 large yellow onions, sliced thin

4 cloves garlic, sliced thin

1 pound button mushrooms, sliced thin

2 tablespoons flour

2 cups beef stock

kosher salt

freshly ground black pepper

2 tablespoons fresh parsley, chopped

1 teaspoon fresh thyme, chopped

½ cup sour cream

1 teaspoon Dijon mustard

In a large saucepot, melt 2 tablespoons of the butter over medium-high heat.

Sauté the beef until it's golden brown, approximately 5 minutes. Add the onions, garlic and mushrooms. Cook until the onions and mushrooms are soft, approximately 5 minutes. Add the flour and cook for 2 minutes. Add the beef stock and cook until the liquid is reduced by half.

Season with salt and pepper, then add the parsley and thyme. Remove the pot from the heat and add the sour cream and Dijon. Stir to combine. Season with more salt and pepper, if necessary, and serve over mashed potatoes, noodles or rice.

LOCALS TASTING ROOM

These fall-off-the-bone-tender short ribs have a very gentle sweetness, which comes from the balsamic vinegar glaze. Be sure to marinate the ribs for 8 to 12 hours before proceeding with the recipe.

21023-A Geyserville Avenue
Geyserville, CA 95441
707-857-4900
www.tastelocalwines.com

SHORT RIBS
in wine & balsamic sauce

chef Dino Bugica, Diavola Pizzeria & Salumeria

Pair with Dark Horse Zinfandel

SERVES 6

1-1/2 cups dry red wine

1 carrot, peeled and sliced

1 leek, trimmed and sliced

1 celery stalk, sliced

6 black peppercorns

2 garlic cloves, halved

1 clove

2 flat-leaf parsley stems

1 spring rosemary

3 pounds short ribs, cut into
  8 pieces

1/4 cup flour

kosher salt and freshly
  ground black pepper

2 to 3 tablespoons vegetable
  oil

1 to 1-1/4 cups beef broth

2 tablespoons balsamic
  vinegar

To a medium saucepan, add the wine, carrot, leek, celery, garlic, peppercorns and clove, and bring to a boil. Reduce the heat so that the wine bubbles gently for a few minutes. Pour the marinade into a bowl, add the parsley stems and rosemary, and set aside to cool.

Place the ribs, meaty side down, in a bowl and pour the cooled marinade over them. Cover and refrigerate the ribs for 8 to 12 hours, turning them over occasionally.

Preheat oven to 300°.

Remove the ribs from the marinade and drain well; reserve the marinade. Season the flour with salt and pepper, and dredge the ribs in the flour mixture, brushing off any excess. In a Dutch oven, heat the oil over medium heat. Brown the ribs well on all sides. After browning, remove the ribs from the pan and set them aside.

Pour the marinade, with all the vegetables and seasonings, into a Dutch oven and bring the mixture to a boil, stirring well and scraping the browned bits from the bottom of the pan. Return the ribs to the pot and add enough stock to almost cover the ribs. Cover the Dutch oven with a lid and place it in the oven. Cook for 3 hours, or until the ribs are very tender and almost falling from the bone. Transfer them to a baking dish and keep warm, covering loosely with foil.

Strain the braising liquid, discarding the vegetables, herbs and spices. Skim off the fat, then return the liquid to the pot and bring the mixture to a boil. Boil until the mixture is reduced to 1 cup, about 3 to 4 minutes. Add the balsamic vinegar and adjust the seasonings, if necessary.

Pour the braising liquid over the ribs and return them to the oven. Cook, uncovered, for 10 to 15 minutes, and serve.

MATRIX WINERY

This recipe was influenced by my travels and working in some of San Francisco's finest restaurants. Good food should be about simple ingredients turned into something extraordinary. This is what this recipe represents for me. Please enjoy!

3291 Westside Road
Healdsburg, CA 95448
707-433-1911
www.matrixwinery.com

roasted lavender honey
DUCK BREAST
with kabocha squash & ras el hanout

chef Eskender Aseged, Radio Africa & Kitchen

Pair with Matrix Bacigalupi Vineyard Russian River Valley Pinot Noir

SERVES 6

SQUASH

2 medium kabocha squash

1/2 teaspoon freshly ground
   pepper

1/2 teaspoon salt

1/2 teaspoon cardamom

1/2 teaspoon ground cinnamon

1/2 teaspoon ginger powder

1 tablespoon parsley, chopped

1/2 teaspoon lemon zest

1/2 teaspoon garlic, pressed

1 tablespoon extra virgin olive oil

1/2 teaspoon honey

DUCK

6 duck breasts

1/2 tablespoon honey

6 sprigs of lavender or 1
   teaspoon dried lavender
   flower

1/2 teaspoon cumin

1/2 teaspoon coriander

1 teaspoon garlic, pressed

juice of 1/2 lemon

pinch of salt and pepper

1 tablespoon extra virgin olive oil

To prepare the squash, preheat the oven to 400°. Bake the squash for about 45 minutes, or until they're soft. Let them cool a little bit, then cut the squash in half and remove the seeds. Scoop out the flesh and place it in a mixing bowl. Add the remaining squash ingredients and mash them thoroughly. Transfer the mixture to a baking pan and reheat it when you're ready to serve.

To prepare the duck, preheat the oven to 350°. Mix all of the ingredients in a bowl, add the duck, and allow the breasts to marinate for at least 20 minutes but not more than 1 day.

Sear the duck, skin side down, on medium high heat for 3 minutes, closely watching to make sure it doesn't burn. (Honey has a tendency to burn on high heat). Flip the duck on the meat side and finish cooking them in the oven for about 6 minutes.

Remove the breasts from the pan and let them rest for about 5 minutes. Slice the duck and place it around the warmed puree of squash.

MARTORANA FAMILY WINERY

This is an old recipe from my Nonni that our family loves. It's very simple and very delicious – the sausages simmer in their own juices. Be sure to caramelize each ingredient separately and finish the dish in the oven. Mangiare bene!

5956 West Dry Creek Road
Healdsburg, CA 95448
707-433-1909
www.martoranafamilywinery.com

salsiccia con peperoni

SLIDERS

chef Gio Martorana

Pair with Martorana Dry Creek Valley Zinfandel

SERVES 4

6 sweet Italian sausages

3 large yellow onions, cut into
wedges

2 yellow bell peppers, cut
into wedges

2 red bell peppers, cut into
wedges

3 cloves garlic, peeled and
smashed

12 small sourdough rolls

extra virgin olive oil,
preferably Olio di Gio

Preheat oven to 400°.

In a thick frying pan, brown the sausages, poking them with a fork so that they release their juices. Halfway through browning, add the smashed garlic cloves.

Transfer the browned sausages and garlic to a baking dish, and leave the sausage fat in the pan. Add the onions to the pan and cook them until they're caramelized. Add the bell peppers and continue to cook, stirring, until the peppers are browned yet still crunchy. Add the peppers and onions to the baking dish with the sausages, and bake, uncovered, for 15 minutes.

To serve, slice the rolls in half, and cut the sausages in half horizontally in "butterfly" fashion. Place a sausage on the bottom bun and add the onions and peppers on top. Drizzle the top bun with Olio di Gio and place it on the onions and peppers.

MAZZOCCO SONOMA WINERY

This lamb recipe is inspired by warm days and travels in Morocco. Good food is simple ingredients turned into something extraordinary!

1400 Lytton Springs Road
Healdsburg, CA 95448
707-431-8159
www.mazzocco.com

ROASTED LEG OF LAMB
with green chermoula aioli

chef Eskender Aseged, Radio Africa & Kitchen

Pair with Mazzocco Briar Dry Creek Valley Zinfandel

SERVES 6

LAMB

3 pounds leg of lamb, fat trimmed

3 sprigs rosemary

½ teaspoon red pepper flakes

juice of 1 lemon

1 tablespoon garlic, minced

½ teaspoon salt

½ teaspoon pepper

AIOLI

1 bunch cilantro, stemmed and chopped finely

½ tablespoon garlic, crushed

juice of 2 lemons

1 teaspoon cumin

1 teaspoon coriander

2 teaspoons salt

2 teaspoons ground black pepper

4 jalapenos, seeded and finely chopped

2 tablespoons mayonnaise

To prepare the lamb, preheat the oven to 350°.

Combine all the ingredients in a large bowl and allow the lamb to marinate for at least 20 minutes. In a well-oiled cast iron pan, sear the lamb over high heat for about 3 minutes. Turn the meat over and place the pan in the preheated oven for 4 to 6 minutes, to finish the cooking. Let the lamb rest for 5 minutes before serving.

To prepare the aioli, place all the ingredients in a blender and puree until the mixture is smooth. Serve the aioli with the lamb.

MEDLOCK AMES

We came up with this recipe for one of our Valentine's Day events, and it was an instant success. When we can, we select as many of the ingredients from our garden as possible. Very easy to make and very tasty, these sliders are perfect for any occasion. Start the recipe one day ahead.

3487 Alexander Valley Road
Healdsburg, CA 95448
707-431-8845
www.medlockames.com

PULLED PORK SLIDERS
with coleslaw

chef Mickey W. Peterson

Pair with Medlock Ames Bell Mountain Ranch Red

MAKES 50 SLIDERS

PORK
3 tablespoons paprika
1 tablespoon garlic powder
2 tablespoons light brown sugar
2 tablespoons dry mustard
2 tablespoons salt, coarse or kosher
5-7 pounds boneless pork shoulder

COLESLAW
1/2 cup mayonnaise
1/3 cup granulated sugar
2-1/2 tablespoons lemon juice
1 tablespoon white vinegar
1/2 tablespoon cider vinegar
1 teaspoon kosher salt
dash of pepper
1/2 teaspoon celery seed
1/2 teaspoon bitters
2 tablespoons onion, pulverized
1-1/2 teaspoons horseradish
10 cups green and purple cabbage,
    shredded
1/4 cup carrot, shredded

SAUCE
3/4 cup cider vinegar
1 cup course ground or brown mustard
1 cup ketchup (preferably homemade)
1/3 cup light brown sugar
2 cloves garlic, smashed
1 teaspoon salt
1 tablespoon molasses
1/2 cup barbecue sauce
2 ounces Medlock Ames Red wine
1/2 teaspoon bitters
black pepper to taste
50 2-inch-diameter Hawaiian rolls

Prep the pork shoulder 1 day in advance. In a large bowl, combine all the dry ingredients, add the pork, and thoroughly rub the mixture into the meat. Cover the bowl and place it in the refrigerator overnight.

The next day, preheat the oven to 300°. Roast the pork on a rack for about 5 to 6 hours, or until the internal temperature reaches 175°. Let the meat rest for at least 15 minutes, discard any fat and gristle, and using 2 forks, pull the pork into shreds.

While the pork roasts, prepare the coleslaw. In a large bowl, whisk together the mayonnaise, sugar, lemon juice, vinegars, salt, pepper, celery seed, bitters, onions and horseradish. Add the chopped cabbage and carrots to the bowl, and mix until the dressing evenly coats the vegetables. Chill the slaw for at least 2 hours.

While the meat is resting, prepare the sauce. Combine all the ingredients in a saucepan and cook on low heat for 1 hour, or until the sauce reaches the desired thickness. Add half of the sauce to the pulled meat, and use the remainder for leftovers, if desired.

To serve the sliders, place a generous amount of the sauced pork and the slaw in each roll; add a bread and butter pickle, if desired.

MERRIAM VINEYARDS

Josh Silvers, famed Sonoma County chef/owner of Petite Syrah and Jackson's Bar and Oven, is the creator of this recipe. The earthiness of the mushrooms and slow braising of the short ribs make them a perfect pairing with our full-bodied Cabernet Sauvignon. The ribs are comforting and delicious when the weather turns chilly. Start the recipe a day in advance.

11654 Los Amigos Road
Healdsburg, CA 95448
707-433-4032
www.merriamvineyards.com

mushroom-braised
SHORT RIBS

chef Josh Silvers, Petite Syrah and Jackson's Bar and Oven

Pair with Merriam Vineyards Cabernet Sauvignon

SERVES 6

6 short rib pieces (4 pounds)

3 tablespoons kosher salt

3 tablespoons canola oil

2 teaspoons porcini
  mushroom powder

2 ribs celery, chopped

2 carrots, peeled and
  chopped

1 yellow onion, chopped

2 tablespoons tomato paste

1/2 cup ruby port

3 cups Cabernet Sauvignon

4 cups beef stock

2 bay leaves

3 sprigs fresh thyme

8-10 ounces wild mushrooms,
  chopped

Rub the meat with the kosher salt, cover, and refrigerate overnight.

The next day, preheat the oven to 300°.

Wipe the salt from the short ribs. Heat the oil over high heat in a large roasting pan. Brown the ribs and let them drain on paper towels.

In the same pan, sauté the porcini powder and vegetables for 5 minutes. Add the tomato paste and cook for 1 minute. Add the port and Cabernet Sauvignon and continue cooking, until the mixture reduces slightly. Add the stock, short ribs, bay leaves and thyme, cover the pan tightly, and bake the meat until it's tender, 3 to 3-1/2 hours.

Transfer the ribs to a plate and cover them loosely with aluminum foil. Stir the cooking liquid, discarding all the solids. Skim and discard the fat. Add the mushrooms to the pan and cook over medium-high heat, stirring occasionally, for 30 minutes. Reduce the heat, then add the short ribs, and continue to cook until the ribs are heated through. Season with salt and pepper to taste, and serve over mashed potatoes.

MOSHIN VINEYARDS

During Oysterpalooza, Amber Moshin discovered this smoked beef brisket tucked inside a sandwich; its flavor seared into her memory like a hot branding iron. Now you can enjoy it with a "Big Red" from Moshin Vineyards – a match made in heaven! Come on; you can't live on Pinot Noir alone.

10295 Westside Road
Healdsburg, CA 95448
707-433-5499
www.moshinvineyards.com

smokin' slow

MOSHIN BRISKET

chef Brandon Guenther, Rocker Oysterfellers & Firefly Fine Catering

Pair with Moshin Carreras Vineyard Dry Creek Valley Zinfandel

SERVES 8

1 4-pound good-quality beef brisket flat, fat still intact

½ cup kosher salt

3 tablespoons ground black pepper

oak chips, wine barrel staves or other hardwood smoking chips – soaked in water for 30 minutes

heatproof thermometer probe

old blanket or towel

plastic ice chest large enough to hold brisket tightly when wrapped with clean blanket or towel

Prepare your cooking apparatus (charcoal or gas grill, vertical or Texas smoker) and heat it to 225°, using indirect heat.

Season the brisket liberally with salt and pepper. Place it in the smoking apparatus, fat side up, directly on the grate. Insert the temperature probe into the thickest part of the meat. Add enough wood chips to the coals or smoking box to create smoke, close the lid, and open the vents 1/4 of the way.

IMPORTANT: Maintain a constant 225° in your smoker, adding more wood chips to maintain the smoke. Cook the brisket 1 hour per pound of meat, approximately 4 hours, until the internal meat temperature reaches 190°. Keep the lid closed to maintain temperature and humidity.

After 4 hours, check the internal temperature. If it's not yet 190°, close the lid and wait approximately 1 minute per degree to rise before checking again. When the brisket is done, remove it from the smoker, wrap it tightly in aluminum foil, and place it in the ice chest lined with the blanket or towel. Close the lid and allow the brisket to rest for at least 1 hour and up to 3.

Remove the brisket from the foil and slice it 1/4-inch thick, perpendicular to the grain. Serve immediately with sides of your choice and Moshin Zinfandel.

MOUNTS FAMILY WINERY

Jude Affronti created this amazing dish for Mounts Family Winery after collaborating with owner Lana Mounts to develop a Persian dish from Lana's family heritage. Lana is a first-generation Russian-American whose grandparents and parents came to the United States by way of Persia (Iran). The influence of Persian cuisine in Lana's upbringing marries beautifully with the rich and elegant wines she and her husband and winemaker, David Mounts, produce from the family's estate vineyards.

3901 Wine Creek Road
Healdsburg, CA 95448
707-292-8148
www.mountswinery.com

KHORESHT FESENJAAN

(persian chicken stew)

chef Jude Affronti, Affronti Wine Bar & Restaurant

Pair with Mounts Cypress Zinfandel

SERVES 4-6

1 pound boneless/skinless chicken thighs

1 teaspoon cardamom, ground

1 teaspoon coriander, ground

1 teaspoon cinnamon, ground

1 teaspoon salt

¼ cup vegetable oil, divided

2 yellow onions, peeled and sliced

½ pound walnuts, coarse ground

4 cups pomegranate juice

Cut the chicken into small cubes, about 1/4 to 1/2 of an inch thick. Toss the chicken cubes with the spices and salt, and set aside. This can be done up to 1 day ahead, but don't add the salt until just before cooking.

In a large, heavy-bottomed stockpot over medium-high heat, add 4 tablespoons of the oil. Add the onions and cook, stirring frequently, until they're soft, about 3 to 5 minutes. Reduce the heat to medium-low and continue cooking, stirring occasionally, until the onions are very tender and light golden in color, about 7 to 10 minutes. Remove the onions from the pan and set aside.

Do not wash the pan. Return it to the heat and add the remaining oil. Add the seasoned chicken, and stir to coat. Allow the chicken to brown lightly before stirring, 2 to 3 minutes per side.

When the chicken is browned on all sides, return the onions to the pan, increase the heat to high, and add the walnuts and pomegranate juice. Bring to a simmer, reduce the heat to low, and cook uncovered, until the chicken is tender and the liquid has reduced by about 1/2.

Serve with white rice and garnish with fresh pomegranate seeds.

Note: If you use a food processor for grinding the walnuts, be careful not to over-process; you don't want walnut "meal."

MUELLER WINERY

No matter how hectic it gets during harvest, our family takes a little time to enjoy the fruits of our labor. A few times during crush, we actually sit down to a hearty meal and a glass of wine. Even though the outside temperatures are usually warm, the cellar is chilly. Chef Shari of Baci Café & Wine Bar delivers us this delicious dish, which we enjoy with our Emily's Cuvée Pinot Noir. The tough part is getting back to work. Be sure to brine the meat the night before you plan to serve it.

6301 Starr Road
Windsor, CA 95492
707-837-7399
www.muellerwine.com

slow roasted

PORK SHOULDER

with creamy polenta & pinot noir reduction

chef Shari Sarabi, Baci Café & Wine Bar

Pair with Mueller Emily's Cuvée Russian River Valley Pinot Noir

SERVES 6

2-1/2 pounds pork shoulder

2 gallons water

2 cups salt

1 cup sugar

1/2 cup whole peppercorns

1 onion, quartered

2 lemons, cut in half

POLENTA

1 tablespoon olive oil

1 medium yellow onion, finely diced

1 tablespoon garlic, minced

1 teaspoon rosemary

3 cups chicken stock

1 cup heavy cream

1/2 cup polenta

1/2 cup grated Parmesan cheese

1/4 pound butter

REDUCTION

1 bottle Mueller Emily's Cuvée Pinot Noir

1 cup rich demi-glace

1 stick butter

salt and pepper to taste

To prepare the pork, add the water, salt, sugar, peppercorns, onions and lemons to a large container. Place the pork shoulder in this brine and refrigerate it overnight.

The next day, preheat the oven to 225° and slow-roast the pork for 9 hours. Remove it from the oven, discard any fat and gristle, and pull the meat apart with 2 forks. Keep it warm.

To prepare the polenta, heat the oil in a Dutch oven and add the onion, garlic and rosemary. Cook until the onions are translucent. Add 1 cup of chicken stock and the cream, and bring to a boil.

Reduce the heat, add the cornmeal and whisk until the mixture is smooth. On low heat, cook the polenta for 45 minutes, adding the remaining chicken stock slowly, so that the polenta does not get thick. Remove the polenta from the heat, and while whisking, add the cheese and butter.

To prepare the Pinot Noir reduction sauce, pour the wine into a saucepan and over low heat, reduce the liquid 1/3. Add the demi-glace, then blend in the butter. Add salt and pepper to taste.

To serve, place the pork on the polenta and drizzle with the Pinot Noir sauce.

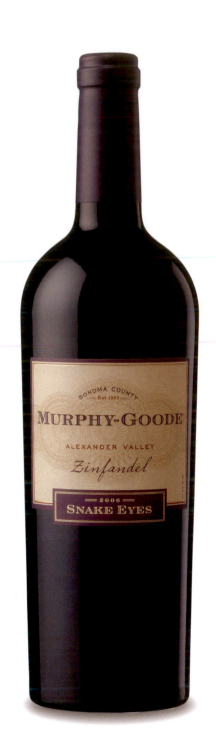

MURPHY-GOODE

Exactly what constitutes a taco varies from region to region in both the United States and Mexico. For our version, we fill our tacos with achiote-rubbed beef, Monterey Jack cheese and sour cream. The combination of smoky beef and salty cheese stands up to the complexity of our Murphy-Goode Snake Eyes Zinfandel.

20 Matheson Street
Healdsburg, CA 95448
707-431-7644
www.murphygoodewinery.com

grilled achiote spiced

SKIRT STEAK TACOS

Recipe by chef Taki Laliotitis

Pair with Murphy-Goode Snake Eyes Zinfandel

MAKES 8 TACOS

2 tablespoons achiote paste

2 tablespoons vegetable oil

1 pound beef skirt steak

kosher salt

1 teaspoon vegetable oil

8 corn tortillas

1/2 cup Monterey Jack
  cheese, grated

1/2 bunch cilantro leaves,
  picked and washed

3 radishes, shaved thin

1/2 cup sour cream

Combine the achiote paste and 2 tablespoons of oil in a bowl and mix thoroughly. Rub the skirt steak with the mixture and season liberally with salt. Grill on both sides over a medium-high mesquite grill, until the beef is medium-rare, approximately 2 to 3 minutes per side. Remove the meat from the grill, cover with foil and let it rest for 5 minutes. Slice the beef very thin, against the grain. Remove any excess fat or sinew. Season with salt to taste.

In a heavy-bottomed pan, heat 1 teaspoon of oil. Lightly toast the tortillas on each side in the oiled pan, wrap them in a clean kitchen towel and keep them warm.

To assemble the tacos, cover half of each tortilla with 1 tablespoon of grated cheese, a small handful of cilantro leaves, 2 ounces of beef, 2 slices radish and 1 tablespoon sour cream. Fold each tortilla in half. Serve hot and enjoy.

RED CAR WINERY

We are indebted to Suzanne Goin, chef/owner of Lucques restaurant in Los Angeles, for giving us permission to use her recipe in this book. We will serve this spectacular duck dish at "A Wine & Food Affair."

8400 Graton Road
Sebastopol, CA 95472
707-829-8500
www.redcarwine.com

GRILLED DUCK BREAST

with farro, cavolo nero & cherry compote

chef Suzanne Goin, Lucques Restaurant

Pair with Red Car Trolley Pinot Noir

SERVES 6

CHERRY COMPOTE

1/2 bunch thyme

2 bay leaf

2 chiles d'arbol

3 star anise

1 cinnamon stick

1 teaspoon black peppercorns

1/4 cup granulated sugar

1/2 cup port

juice of 2 oranges

1-1/2 cups pitted cherries

1 tablespoon unsalted butter

DUCK

1 tablespoon juniper berries

6 single pekin duck breasts, 6
    to 8 ounces each (or 4 larger
    muscovy breasts)

1 tablespoon thyme leaves

1 pound cavolo nero (black kale),
    cleaned, center ribs removed

1/2 cup extra virgin olive oil

1/2 sprig rosemary

1 chiles d'arbol, crumbled

1 cup onion, sliced

2 cloves garlic, thinly sliced

2 cups farro

To prepare the cherry compote, make a sachet of cheesecloth and put in it the thyme, bay leaves, chiles, star anise, cinnamon and peppercorns. Place the sugar and 1 cup of water in a medium saucepan. Bring the liquid to a boil over medium-high heat, and add the port, orange juice and the sachet. Turn the heat down to a simmer and add the cherries. Poach the cherries 8 to 10 minutes, until they're just tender; they should retain their shape.

Strain the cherries over a bowl, and return the liquid to the saucepan. Cook the liquid over high heat about 5 minutes, until it has reduced by 2/3. It should be slightly thickened and have a glossy sheen. Strain the liquid and let cool. Stir in the cherries, and season to taste with salt and pepper. When you are ready to serve the compote, heat it in a saucepan and swirl in the butter.

To prepare the duck breasts, pound the juniper berries in a mortar until they're coarsely ground. Score the skin of the duck breasts with a sharp knife, and season with the juniper berries and thyme leaves. Cover, and refrigerate at least 4 hours, preferably overnight.

Bring a large pot of heavily salted water to a boil over high heat. Blanch the cavolo nero in the water for 2 minutes. Drain, let cool, and squeeze out the excess water. Return the pot to the stove over medium heat for 2 minutes. Pour in 1/4 cup of the olive oil and add the rosemary sprig and chile. Let them sizzle in the oil for about 1 minute. Turn the heat down to medium-low, and add the onion. Season with 1/2 teaspoon of salt and a pinch of freshly ground pepper. Cook 2 minutes and stir in the sliced garlic. Continue cooking another 5 to 7 minutes, stirring often with a wooden spoon, until the onion is soft and starting to color.

Add the cavolo nero and 2 more tablespoons of olive oil, stirring to coat the greens in the oil and onion. Season with a heaping 1/4 teaspoon salt, and cook the greens slowly over low heat for about 30 minutes, stirring often, until they turn a dark, almost black color and get slightly crispy on the edges. Turn off the heat and set the pot aside. When the ingredients have cooled, remove the rosemary and chile.

While the cavolo nero is cooking, cook the farro in boiling, well-salted water for about 30 minutes or until it's tender. Drain the farro, and spread it on a baking sheet to cool.

Light the grill 30 minutes before cooking, and remove the duck from the refrigerator to allow it to come to room temperature. Season the duck with salt and pepper. Place the duck breasts, skin side down, on the cooler half of the grill. As they cook, rotate the breasts a quarter-turn every 2 minutes, to allow the fat to render and the skin to crisp. Turn the breasts over, and cook until the duck is medium-rare and still springy to the touch. Remove the meat from the heat, and let it rest for 5 minutes on a wire rack set over a baking sheet.

To finish the farro, heat a large sauté pan over high heat for 2 minutes. Swirl in 2 tablespoons olive oil, add the farro, and season with salt and pepper. Sauté, stirring continuously, for 3 to 4 minutes, until the farro is slightly crispy. Add the cavolo nero and stir well to combine. Taste for seasoning and divide the farro between 6 plates. Slice the duck breasts and place them over the farro. Spoon the cherries over the top and around the plate.

SUNCE WINERY

This is a fusion of two of Sunce winemaker Frane Franicevic's favorite dishes: Croatian moussaka and American-style lasagna.

1839 Olivet Road
Santa Rosa, CA 95401
707-526-9463
www.suncewinery.com

frane's
MOUSSAKA LASAGNA
chef Denise Stewart

Pair with Sunce Zemlja's Blend

SERVES 6-8

LASAGNA

1 medium eggplant

1 red pepper

1 medium potato

2 ounces olive oil

1/2 cup carrots, finely diced

1 large onion, diced

2 pounds lean organic ground
beef

3 fresh tomatoes, diced

2 large garlic cloves, crushed

1 beef bouillon cube

1 teaspoon Italian seasoning

1/2 teaspoon rock salt

1 teaspoon coarse black pepper

1 pinch nutmeg

1 pinch cinnamon

1/2 cup mozzarella cheese

8 no-boil lasagna noodles

BECHEMEL SAUCE

2 1/2 tablespoons flour

1/4 cup butter

2 cups hot milk

1/2 cup Parmesan cheese, grated

1 cup ricotta cheese

2 eggs, beaten

Preheat oven to 400°.

To prepare the lasagna, partially peel the eggplant so it looks striped. Cut it into 1/4-inch-thick rounds and brush each side with olive oil. Roast in the oven for 15 minutes. Leave the oven on.

Meanwhile, grill the red pepper, skin side up, until it's blackened. Peel off the skin and dice the flesh. Peel and cut the potato into 1/4-inch rounds and quickly par-boil the slices so that the outer rim just begins to soften. Drain the potatoes.

Sauté the red pepper, carrot and onion in the olive oil until the onions are translucent. Add the beef and fry. Add the tomatoes, garlic, bouillon cube, Italian seasoning, salt, black pepper, nutmeg and cinnamon; turn the heat way down after the meat has browned.

To prepare the bechamel sauce, in a small saucepan, mix the flour and butter over low heat until a thick paste forms. Making sure it doesn't burn. Keep spreading the paste around for a couple minutes, until the flour cooks off. Slowly add the hot milk, little by little, stirring continuously. Add the Parmesan and ricotta, and keep stirring. Let the mixture cool for a few minutes before stirring in the beaten eggs.

To assemble the lasagna, soak the lasagna noodles in hot water for a few minutes, then drain. In a deep casserole, place the potato rounds, then a layer of lasagna noodles. Next add a layer of eggplant rounds, then half the ground beef mixture, then the mozzarella. Add another layer of noodles, eggplant rounds, then the rest of the ground beef.

Pour the bechamel over the top of the lasagna and bake it in the oven (400°) for 40 minutes, or until it's lightly browned along the edges. Allow it to cool (this sets the top layer of "custard") for 20 minutes before cutting the lasagna into squares and serving. Some guests might like to add Tabasco sauce to their serving.

TAFT STREET WINERY

We served these sandwiches at a winery party recently and they were a big hit. Most of the work can be done ahead of time, and assembly is quick and easy. Marinate the pork overnight before continuing with the recipe.

2030 Barlow Lane
Sebastopol, CA 95472
707-823-2049
www.taftstreetwinery.com

PULLED PORK SANDWICHES
with slaw

Pair with Taft Street Russian River Valley Pinot Noir

SERVES 12

PORK
2 teaspoons ground cumin
1 teaspoon ground coriander
2 teaspoons salt
2 teaspoons chili powder
3 pounds pork butt or
   shoulder, trimmed and cut
   into 1-1/2-inch cubes
1/4 cup olive oil
1/2 cup red wine vinegar
1 tablespoon honey
1/2 cup chicken stock
1 onion, diced
12 kaiser rolls

SLAW
1/2 cup distilled white vinegar
4 tablespoons sugar
4 tablespoons vegetable oil
2-1/2 teaspoons dry mustard
1 teaspoon celery seeds
1 medium cabbage, thinly
   shredded
1 large red onion, thinly sliced
2 carrots, shredded

To prepare the pork, combine the first 4 ingredients in a small bowl. Rub the mixture into the pork pieces and place them in a container. Cover and refrigerate overnight.

The next day, in a sauté pan, brown the pork in olive oil and set aside. Add the vinegar, honey and stock to the pan, scraping up the bits at the bottom. Add the onion and bring the mixture to a boil. Lower the heat to a simmer, add the pork and cook until the cubes are tender, about 90 minutes. Let the meat cool, then shred it by hand.

Meanwhile, prepare the slaw by combining the vinegar, sugar, oil, mustard and celery seeds in a medium saucepan. Stir and bring to a boil. Remove the pan from the heat and season the mixture with salt and pepper. Allow the dressing to cool.

In a large bowl, combine the cabbage, onion and carrots. Add the dressing, toss, cover and refrigerate for at least 2 hours.

To serve, split the kaiser rolls and toast them briefly. Place 2 heaping tablespoons of slaw on the bottom half of each roll, and cover with 2 heaping tablespoons of pork. Add the top half of the roll, wrap the sandwich in a large paper napkin, and serve.

TERROIRS ARTISAN WINES

Chef Dino Bugica, winemaker Kerry Damskey and John Piccetti, from the founding family of Columbus Salami Co., created this marmalade for pork roast, which reflects Geyserville's Italian heritage and passion for great wine and food. In southern Italy, the sweet red Tropea onion of Calabria is typically used for making the full-flavored marmalade. Serve it with your favorite pork roast dish. Marmellata di Cipolle Rosse is also delicious spread on bread and topped with slices of salumi.

21001 Geyserville Avenue
Geyserville, CA 95441
707-857-4101
www.terroirsartisanwines.com

MARMELLATA DI CIPOLLE

rosse for roast pork

Pair with Terroirs Artisan Petite Sirah

MAKES 3 TO 4 CUPS

½ cup olive oil

6 large red onions, thinly
  sliced

1 cup sugar

2 cups red wine vinegar

1 teaspoon mustard seeds
  (optional)

1 tablespoon orange zest,
  grated (optional)

freshly ground black pepper

In a large sauté pan, warm the olive oil over low heat. Add the onions and cook, stirring often, until they're softened, about 20 minutes. Add the sugar, vinegar, mustard seeds (if using) and orange zest (if using) and simmer until almost all the liquid has evaporated and the onions are syrupy, about 20 minutes longer.

Remove the pan from the heat and season the marmalade with lots of pepper. Let it cool to room temperature and serve.

The marmalade will keep, tightly covered, in the refrigerator for up to 2 months. Bring it to room temperature for serving.

TOAD HOLLOW VINEYARDS

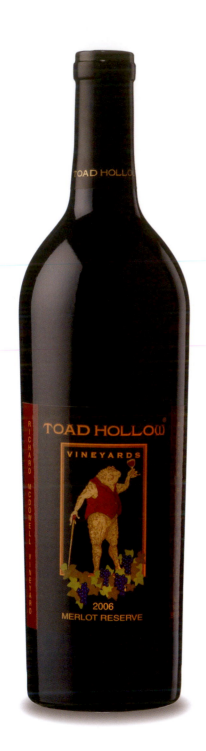

This rich, cheesy and delicious dish was invented by Debbie Rickards from our tasting room. She just knew all of these ingredients would blend, balance and melt together beautifully!

409-A Healdsburg Avenue
Healdsburg, CA 95448
707-431-8667
www.toadhollow.com

POLENTA

with gorgonzola & mascarpone served with marinara sauce

chef Debbie Rickards

vegi

Pair with Toad Hollow Richard McDowell Vineyard Merlot

SERVES 6-8

MARINARA

extra virgin olive oil
1/2 onion, chopped
1 teaspoon red pepper flakes
2 tablespoon dry oregano
4-6 cloves garlic, chopped
2 28-ounce cans Cento San
  Marzano whole tomatoes
fresh basil leaves

POLENTA

2-1/2 cups water
2 cups vegetable or chicken
  stock
3 large sprigs fresh sage
1 teaspoon salt
1 cup dry yellow polenta
1/2 cup mascarpone (or cream
  cheese)
1/2 cup Gorgonzola cheese
2 tablespoons unsalted butter
fresh ground pepper to taste
6-10 fresh sage leaves,
  slivered (optional)
Parmesan cheese, grated

To prepare the marinara sauce, heat the olive oil in a sauté pan, add the onion, and cook until the onion is soft but not browned. Add the red pepper flakes and oregano. Sauté for 3 to 5 minutes. Add the garlic and cook 1 minute. Break up the canned tomatoes a bit with a fork and add them to the onion mixture. Add a few basil leaves and cook for 15 minutes. Add more fresh basil just before serving.

To prepare the polenta, in a large pot, boil the first 4 ingredients for 3 minutes. Remove the sage sprigs. Add the polenta slowly by the handful, stirring with a wooden spoon while adding. Cook the polenta over medium heat for 15 to 20 minutes, until the mixture starts to pull from the pan when stirred. Add the mascarpone, gorgonzola and butter, and stir until melted. Add the pepper, slivered sage and Parmesan.

Serve the polenta warm, with topped with the marinara sauce.

TOPEL WINERY

Who would have known that my grandmother's favorite Sunday meal (we begged her to make these almost every week!) would taste so delicious 50-plus years later, with our Estate Reserve Cabernet? Thank you, Mettie Bybee Frisch.

125 Matheson Street
Healdsburg, CA 95448
707-433-4116
www.topelwines.com

mettie's marvelous & memorable
MEATBALLS

chef Donnis Topel

Pair with Topel Estate Reserve Cabernet Sauvignon

SERVES 8

5 tablespoons olive oil

3 medium yellow onions, finely diced

salt

freshly ground pepper

2 pounds ground veal

2-$\frac{1}{2}$ tablespoons fresh parsley, finely chopped

3 tablespoons freshly grated Parmesan cheese

3 large eggs

$\frac{1}{2}$ cup bread crumbs

15 small artichokes (2-$\frac{1}{2}$ pounds)

12 ounces cherry tomatoes, peeled

4 cloves garlic, finely chopped

$\frac{2}{3}$ cup green olives, coarsely chopped

2 tablespoons fresh sage leaves, coarsely chopped

2-$\frac{1}{2}$ tablespoons lemon juice

1 cup chicken broth

Warm 3 tablespoons of the olive oil in a sauté pan. Add the onions, salt and pepper them lightly, and cook over moderate heat for 8 minutes, until the onions are softened. Do not let them brown.

Meanwhile, put the veal in a mixing bowl and add the parsley, Parmesan, eggs and bread crumbs. Remove $\frac{1}{3}$ cup of the onions from the pan and add them to the bowl with the veal. Season the mixture with 1 teaspoon salt and $\frac{1}{4}$ teaspoon ground pepper, and mix thoroughly. Form the veal into 16 meatballs, each weighing about 2 ounces, and set them aside on a plate.

Transfer the remaining onions to a large baking dish. Remove the outer leaves of the artichokes until you reach the pale green heart. Trim the pointed end of the heart, cut off the stem and pare away the tough green portion surrounding the artichoke bottom. Cut the artichokes in quarters and place them in a bowl of acidulated water as you work.

Preheat the oven to 350°.

Warm the remaining 2 tablespoons of oil in a 12-inch cast iron pan. When the oil is hot, add the meatballs and brown them all over lightly, allowing 1-$\frac{1}{2}$ minutes per side. Set the meatballs in the baking dish on the bed of onions.

Drain the artichokes. Combine the artichokes with the tomatoes, garlic, olives, sage and lemon juice. Season with $\frac{1}{2}$ teaspoon salt and a grinding of pepper. Mix well and distribute the vegetable mixture around the meatballs. Pour the broth over the dish, cover tightly with foil, and bake in the oven for 1 hour. Transfer the meatballs and vegetables to a large platter, pour some of the juices over them, and serve. They're delicious with fresh noodles tossed with butter and Parmesan.

VML WINERY

This is the inaugural "A Wine & Food Affair" at our winery, and this recipe is important to us! Sylvia bought a new Weber grill and started the fire. I had my doubts, but they were erased when I smelled the smoky mesquite getting white-hot. The deal was sealed when Sylvia delicately covered steaming slices of juicy, seasoned tender pork with the tart, sweet and intense cherry sauce. This pork has panache!

4035 Westside Road
Healdsburg, CA 95448
707-431-4404
www.vmlwine.com

PORK WITH PANACHE

chef Sylvia Hurst

Pair with VML Russian River Valley Pinot Noir

SERVES 4

1 tablespoon cornstarch

3 tablespoons butter, room temperature

1 tablespoon Dijon mustard

1-1/2 pounds pork tenderloin

2 teaspoons lemon-pepper seasoning

1-1/2 cups VML Pinot Noir

1 cup dried cherries, chopped

3 tablespoons cherry preserves

salt to taste

1/4 to 1/2 cup chicken stock

In a small bowl, combine the cornstarch, butter and mustard and blend until it's smooth. Set aside.

Sprinkle the pork with lemon-pepper seasoning. Prepare the grill with mesquite charcoal. Heat the wine in a pan and reduce down to $3/4$ cup. Add the cherries and the preserves; stir and cook for 2 minutes. Add the cornstarch mixture and salt to the pan and cook, stirring, until the sauce thickens. Add chicken stock for the desired thickness of the sauce.

Roast the tenderloin over very hot mesquite charcoal for 4 to 5 minutes on each side. Slice the pork and serve with the cherry/Pinot sauce. Accompany with steamed wild and brown rice.

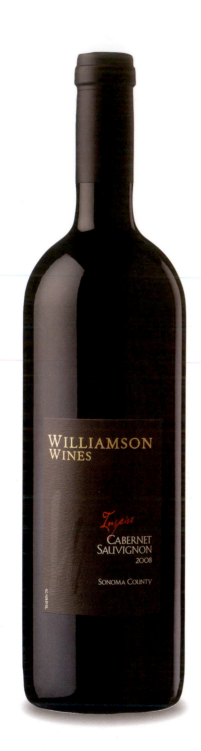

WILLIAMSON WINES

There are few dishes as versatile as the hamburger and here, chef Bill Williamson raises it to gourmet status! The secret to gourmet cooking is using high-quality, fresh ingredients as close to the day they were harvested as possible. Ask your local butcher to coarse-grind the beef freshly for you – round, chuck sirloin or a combination. Do not ask for lean meat, as you need a fat content of 15% or more. Purchase the beef the day you intend to grill it.

134 Matheson Street
Healdsburg, CA 95448
707-433-1500
www.williamsonwines.com

INSPIRE BURGERS

chef Bill Williamson

Pair with Williamson Wines Inspire Cabernet Sauvignon

SERVES 4

1 bottle Williamson Merlot

¼ cup shallots, minced

9 tablespoons unsalted butter, room temperature

2 teaspoons golden brown sugar

1-½ pounds ground beef

1 tablespoon fresh rosemary, minced

1 teaspoon salt

½ teaspoon ground black pepper

vegetable oil

1 cup coarsely grated Irish cheddar cheese, packed

4 half-inch-thick squares focaccia bread, cut horizontally in half

2 cups arugula

In a medium sauté pan, boil the wine and shallots until the mixture is reduced to ³/₄ cup. Remove the pan from the heat and transfer the reduction to a small bowl. Set aside.

Add 1 tablespoon of the butter and the brown sugar, and whisk the reduction until the butter melts and the sugar dissolves. Cool the mixture completely before adding the ground beef. Mix the remaining 8 tablespoons of butter and the rosemary in a small bowl. Set aside.

Heat the grill to medium-high. Mix the beef, salt, pepper and ¼ cup of the wine-shallot mixture in a bowl. Form the meat into 4 5-inch squares or rounds, about 1 inch thick. Make the meat patties slightly larger than the bread, and don't pack the meat too firmly, just enough so that it holds together on the grill. Brush the grill rack with oil and grill the burgers until they're brown on the bottom, about 3 minutes. Flip the burgers and brush the tops with wine-shallot mixture. Continue grilling until the burgers are cooked to the desired doneness, turning and brushing occasionally with wine-shallot mixture, about 4 minutes longer for medium-rare.

After the last turn, add the cheese to the tops of the burgers and cook until the cheese melts. Spread the cut sides of the bread with the rosemary butter. On low heat, grill the slices, cut side down, until they're golden, about 2 minutes.

To serve, arrange the bread, grilled side up, on plates. Top the bottom halves with burgers and arugula, and cover with the top halves of the bread.

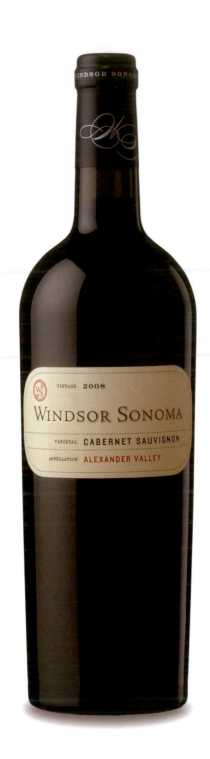

WINDSOR VINEYARDS

Wild mushrooms and whole juniper berries give these stick-to-your-ribs short ribs a slightly exotic yet comforting flavor.

308 B Center Street
Healdsburg, CA 95448
707-921-2893
www.windsorvineyards.com

wild mushroom & juniper berry
SHORT RIBS
with harvest rice

chef Helena Gustavsson Giesea

Pair with Windsor Sonoma Cabernet Sauvignon

SERVES 4

SHORT RIBS

8 short ribs, bone-in (3 pounds)
1-1/2 tablespoons salt
2 teaspoons ground black pepper
2 tablespoons olive oil
1/2 cup yellow onion, diced
1 tablespoon garlic, chopped
1/2 cup wild mushrooms (porcini,
   black trumpet, chanterelle),
   chopped
1-1/2 cups Windsor Sonoma
   Cabernet
1-1/2 cups water
2 tablespoons whole juniper berries
1 tablespoon whole allspice
1 tablespoon whole black peppercorns
1 tablespoon fresh rosemary
2 tablespoons tomato paste
1/2 cup heavy cream
1 to 2 teaspoons salt

HARVEST RICE

2 cups basmati rice
1/4 cup wild rice blend
2-1/2 cups water
2 teaspoons salt
1 tablespoon paprika
1/4 teaspoon ground black pepper
1 tablespoon fresh garlic, chopped

Preheat oven to 275°.

Sprinkle the short ribs with salt and pepper. Add the oil to a sauté pan and brown the ribs on all sides over medium heat. Remove the ribs from the pan and place them in a greased ovenproof pan.

In the same sauté pan, cook the onion, garlic and mushrooms. Add the wine, water, spices, herbs and tomato paste, stir, and bring the mixture to a boil. Remove the sauce from the heat and pour it over the short ribs. Cover the pan with foil and roast the ribs in the oven for 3 hours.

When the meat is tender, remove it from the oven. Strain the pan juices into a saucepan and simmer the liquid until it's reduced by half. Add the cream and season with salt, if necessary.

To prepare the Harvest Rice, place all the ingredients in a large saucepan and bring the mixture to a boil. Stir, cover, and reduce the heat to a low simmer. Cook for 15 to 20 minutes, or until the liquid has evaporated. Remove the pan from the direct heat and let it stand for 10 to 20 minutes, with the lid on. Serve the rice as an accompaniment to the ribs.

DESSERTS

Torrone - Italian Nougat

**Flourless Dark Chocolate Cupcakes with
Petite Sirah-Infused Honey**

Delectable Cheesecake Fudge Brownies

BATTAGLINI ESTATE WINERY

Torrone is a traditional Christmas candy in Italy; being Italian, we enjoy this sweet treat year-round, but particularly in winter. To make handling the sticky nougat mixture easier, you can line the cake pans with edible rice paper before adding the nougat. Place rice paper sheets on top as well. Edible rice paper can be found in Asian food markets, gourmet stores and some supermarkets.

2948 Piner Road
Santa Rosa, CA 95401
707-578-4091
www.battagliniwines.com

TORRONE
(italian nougat)

chef Lucia Battaglini

vegi

Pair with Battaglini Rosato

MAKES 50 PIECES

1 cup honey

2 tablespoons corn syrup

2 egg whites

1 cup sugar

2 tablespoons water

¼ cup butter

1 teaspoon almond extract

1 teaspoon vanilla extract

2 cups whole almonds

2-⅓ cups whole hazelnuts,
   toasted

In a double boiler, place the honey and the corn syrup. Heat the mixture until it boils, stirring constantly with a wooden spoon.

In a separate bowl, beat the egg whites until they're stiff. Add the whites to the honey and continue to stir.

In a heavy saucepan, bring the sugar and water to a boil and cook, stirring continuously, until the mixture is caramelized. Add the honey mixture and blend well. Add the butter, almond extract and vanilla extract, and continue to cook, stirring, until the mixture reaches 240° (test with a candy thermometer).

Remove the nougat from the heat and add the nuts. Mix well. Quickly pour the mixture into 2 oiled 8-inch-square cake pans, and let cool for 20 minutes. Cut the nougat into pieces and wrap them in waxed paper.

FOPPIANO VINEYARDS

We've produced wine in the Russian River Valley for more than 100 years, and Petite Sirah is our flagship varietal. It's a great match for chocolate-based dishes, particularly these flourless mini-cakes. The Petite Sirah-infused honey further connects the cupcakes to the wine.

12707 Old Redwood Highway
Healdsburg, CA 95448
707-433-7272
www.foppiano.com

flourless dark chocolate

CUPCAKES

with petite sirah-infused honey

chef Tim Vallery, Peloton Catering

vegi

Pair with Foppiano Estate Petite Sirah

MAKES 50 MINI-CUPCAKES

HONEY INFUSION

1 750-ml bottle Foppiano
  Estate Petite Sirah

1/4 cup granulated sugar

2 cups wildflower honey

CUPCAKES

7 ounces dark chocolate, at
  least 65% cocoa

3/4 cup unsalted butter,
  coarsely chopped

1/2 cup sugar

3 tablespoons dark cocoa
  powder

1/2 teaspoon kosher salt

1 teaspoon black pepper,
  freshly ground

5 eggs, separated

4 teaspoons vanilla extract

3 tablespoons Petite Sirah
  Infused Honey

Preheat oven to 350°.

To prepare the infused honey, in a stainless steel saucepan, bring the Petite Sirah and sugar to a simmer. Let the mixture reduce by two-thirds of its volume. Add the honey and continue to reduce until it has a syrup-like consistency. The slower you reduce the mixture, the more fruit character it will retain.

To prepare the cupcakes, place liners in a mini-cupcake pan. Over a large double boiler, melt the chocolate and butter together.

In a small bowl, combine the sugar, cocoa powder, salt and pepper. When the chocolate is melted, remove it from the heat and let it rest for about 5 minutes.

Whisk in the 5 egg yolks, vanilla and Petite Sirah honey. Sift in the sugar and cocoa powder mixture, continuously whisking.

In a mixer, whip the 5 egg whites to soft peaks. Fold one-third of the whites into the chocolate mixture, then slowly and carefully fold in the remaining mixture. Over-mixing will break the egg whites.

Spoon the batter into the cupcake liners, and bake the cakes until they are firm but not completely dry in the middle, about 15 minutes. It is normal for them to settle in the middle. Allow them to cool.

To serve, drizzle a small amount of the honey infusion over the cupcakes.

TRENTADUE WINERY

There is no better pick-me-up than chocolate, and when the Trentadue crew needs a midday jump start, we go to the life force ... chocolate brownies! Chocolate is the ultimate attitude adjuster; with one bite of this brownie, we transcend to the land of wine and good times.

19170 Geyserville Avenue
Geyserville, CA 95441

707-433-3104
www.trentadue.com

delectable cheesecake

FUDGE BROWNIES

chef Randi Kauppi, Oui Cater

vegi

Pair with Trentadue Chocolate Amore

MAKES 24 2-INCH BY 2-INCH PIECES

BROWNIE

2 cups sugar

4 ounces unsweetened
  baking chocolate

8 ounces butter

4 egg yolks, slightly beaten

1 cup sifted flour

1 teaspoon vanilla

4 egg whites, beaten to stiff
  peaks

TOPPING

8 ounces cream cheese,
  softened

1 cup sugar

1 teaspoon vanilla

½ cup sour cream

3 eggs

Preheat oven to 325°.

To prepare the brownies, put the sugar in a mixing bowl. In a small saucepan, melt the chocolate and butter together over low heat and stir until blended. Add the chocolate mixture to the sugar and mix well. Add the beaten egg yolks and mix again. Add the flour and vanilla, blend well, then fold the mixture into the beaten egg whites.

Spread the batter into a 9-inch by 13-inch pan coated with cooking spray. Place it in the oven for approximately 25 minutes, or until the top is shiny and the center is almost set.

Meanwhile, prepare the topping. With a mixer, beat the cream cheese, sugar and vanilla in a large bowl. Add the sour cream and mix well. Add 1 egg at a time, mixing on low speed after each egg is added, until just blended. Gently pour the topping mixture over the brownie layer in the pan.

Bake the topped brownie for 40 minutes, or until the center is almost set. Run a knife around the rim of the pan to loosen the sides, and let the brownie cool.

Refrigerate the brownie for 4 hours, then cut into squares and serve.

RECIPE INDEX
by winery & lodging

THE WINERIES

RECIPE INDEX
by winery & lodging

THE WINERIES continued

RECIPE INDEX
by winery & lodging

THE WINERIES continued

RECIPE INDEX
by winery & lodging

NEW HEIGHTS...

Now in its 34th year, the Wine Road has grown from the nine founding winery members to a spirited collection of 190! These world-class wine producers are joined by 56 lodging properties throughout the Alexander, Dry Creek and Russian River valleys of Northern Sonoma County.

Our increased membership is not the only change. In the past few months, we have launched a brand-new website with more information than ever, to help visitors plan their Wine Road adventures. We even have a link to help you connect with our winery members when they are in your area for a special tasting opportunity. For those times when you're already on the "Road" and seeking information, just download our new free iPhone app – iWineRoad.

Wine Road is an easy drive, about one hour north of the Golden Gate Bridge. We enjoy the grandeur of the Pacific Ocean, stately redwoods, picturesque towns and rolling vineyards, all easily accessed along quiet country roads. If you live locally, we hope you treat yourself to a staycation and enjoy the bounty in your backyard. We think you'll agree: Wine Road is...Heaven Condensed.

The Golden Ticket...

The Wine Road now offers a great way to save $$ when you visit our member wineries and lodgings: "Ticket to the Wine Road."

Log onto wineroad.com and click on the TICKET link to see the list of wineries and lodgings that are participating in the program. You can buy a one-day pass for $25 or a three-day pass for $50. When you place your order, simply select the dates you want to use the pass. Currently, 70 wineries and 12 lodgings have special offers, which can include complimentary tastings, barrel tastings and other fun offers for "Ticket" holders. When you order, please note that Wine Road event weekends are blacked out, and that the "Ticket" will not work for groups of eight or more.

So Much To Share...

Don't miss out on Wine Road news. We share our insider news, stories, specials and contests online. We love hearing from you and having a forum where you can share your photos, comments and suggestions with other Wine Road guests. Stay in the loop with Facebook, Twitter and our weekly blog.

ANNUAL WINE ROAD EVENTS

Winter Wineland
January - Martin Luther King Jr. Birthday Weekend

Wine ~ Art ~ Education! This is a great opportunity to meet winemakers and taste limited-production wines. Enjoy a weekend of wine tasting, winemaker chats, winery tours and seminars. Each participating winery will either feature an artist for the weekend or offer some type of wine education.

Tickets are available in advance, online: $45 for the weekend, $35 for Sunday only, and $5 for designated drivers. Once online tickets sales end, prices at the door are $55 weekend, $45 Sunday only and $5 designated drivers. Online tickets go on sale in mid-November at www.wineroad.com.

Barrel Tasting
March - First two weekends

Pack a picnic and join us for this extraordinary tasting opportunity – as the name says, you'll sample wine directly from the barrel! This is your chance to get into the cellar of more than 100 wineries, taste barrel samples and talk with winemakers. It's also an opportunity to purchase "futures," often at a discount. Come back to the winery after the wine is bottled (typically 12-16 months later) and pick up your purchase. The production of many member wineries is so limited that buying "futures" is your only chance to obtain the wine you like. Again, this is not a food event, so we encourage you to pack a picnic to enjoy your barrel tasting adventure.

Tickets are available in advance, online, beginning in mid-January: $30 per person, per weekend. Once online tickets sales end, prices at the door are $40 per person, per weekend. There is no charge for designated drivers, but they are not allowed to sample ANY wine.

A Wine & Food Affair
November - The first full weekend

Our premier event: A full weekend of wine and food pairings, complete with the current volume of our "Tasting Along the Wine Road" cookbook and event logo glass. All participating wineries will have a recipe for a favorite dish in the cookbook, which they will prepare both days for you to sample, paired with the perfect wine. Many Wine Road lodgings also provide recipes for inclusion in the cookbook.

Tickets are available in advance, online: $70 for the weekend, $50 for Sunday only and $30 for designated drivers. Online tickets go on sale in early September at www.wineroad.com. There are NO tickets sold at the door for this event.

For details on these annual Wine Road events
and other member winery events visit
www.wineroad.com

OUR AVAs
(AMERICAN VITICULTURAL AREAS)

The mission of Wine Road is to increase awareness of the Alexander,
Dry Creek and Russian River valleys through education and marketing, and promoting
Sonoma County as the year-round wine country destination.

To that end, we've included some general information about the three AVAs that we represent in Northern Sonoma County, California

Alexander Valley

Total acres: 32,536 • Vineyard acres: 15,000 • Number of wineries: 49, growing 23 grape varieties

This valley is named for the 19th-century pioneer Cyrus Alexander, explorer of Northern Sonoma County and resident of the area. Alexander Valley flanks the Russian River from Cloverdale to Healdsburg. Along the heavily graveled benchlands, one finds world-class Cabernet Sauvignon grapes. Considered one of the most diverse grapegrowing regions in California, the valley is also planted to Chardonnay, Zinfandel, Merlot, Sauvignon Blanc and other varieties, which prosper on the long, undulating valley floor and hillsides.

Forty years ago, prunes and walnuts reigned supreme in the Alexander Valley, and the flatlands were dotted with bovine herds. Today, the lowlands produce Chardonnays that achieve a rich and flavorful ripeness. The warmer northern end of the valley favors Cabernet Sauvignon, Zinfandel, Merlot and newcomers like French Syrah and Italian Sangiovese. Vineyards that scale the hillsides surrounding the valley floor provide grapes with deep and complex flavors. Hunt around and you can also still find some of the juiciest, most succulent prunes you've ever tasted.

Dry Creek Valley
Total acres: 78,387 • Vineyard acres: 10,000 • Number of wineries: 81, growing 26 grape varieties

Dry Creek Valley's history of grapegrowing and winemaking is among the longest in California, with roots beginning more than 135 years ago. The precise blend of climate, soil and exposure that produces grapes of singular quality and character is the true allure of the region.

The valley is approximately 16 miles long and 2 miles wide. It is framed on the western edge by rugged mountain ridges rimmed with redwoods and evergreens. The climate reflects both coastal and inland influences and is classified as Region II on the UC Davis scale. The proximity to the ocean is tempered by the intervening coastal hills breached by the Russian River. While Dry Creek Valley experiences coastal cooling in the late afternoon during summer, fog rarely enters the valley until after nightfall. The climate is warmer in the north and cooler in the south, allowing for diversity of grapegrowing.

Dry Creek Valley is recognized as a premium winegrowing region in California, and Zinfandel is the signature varietal. However, the diversity of the soil encourages the production of a broad range of top-quality Bordeaux and Mediterranean grape varieties.

Russian River Valley
Total acres: 126,600 • Vineyard acres: 10,000 • Number of wineries: 130, growing 30 grape varieties

What makes Russian River Valley stand out is its climate. This low-lying flat plain extends south and west of Healdsburg as it winds its way along the Russian River and descends to meet the Pacific at Jenner, then makes it way toward the Golden Gate Bridge, ending about 55 miles north of this landmark. This area thrives from the coastal influences of the Pacific Ocean, which makes it an exceptional place for growing cool-climate grapes like Pinot Noir and Chardonnay.

The Russian River Valley is so expansive that it has two smaller appellations within it: Green Valley and Chalk Hill. Green Valley is one of the smallest appellations in the county, nestled in the southwest corner of the Russian River Valley. This area is greatly affected by the cooling coastal elements, which benefit the cool-climate grapes that flourish in these conditions. Chalk Hill, named for the volcanic soil that makes up the area, is a unique little gem known for its outstanding wines. By being situated in the northwest corner of Russian River Valley, it has warmer temperatures that allow Merlot and Cabernet Sauvignon to thrive.

Russian River Valley Chardonnays are exceptional, slightly more lean and refined than those of Alexander Valley, yet the fruit is still developed enough to sustain months in oak barrels, creating depth and complexity. Pinot Noir brought this area international acclaim. Whereas most red wines focus on flavor, Pinot Noir is about an alluring, sensual, velvety mouth-feel. It is a textural delight that can only be found where morning fog turns to warm afternoons, so that grape maturity is achieved without loss of depth and suppleness.

OUR AVAs
(AMERICAN VITICULTURAL AREAS)

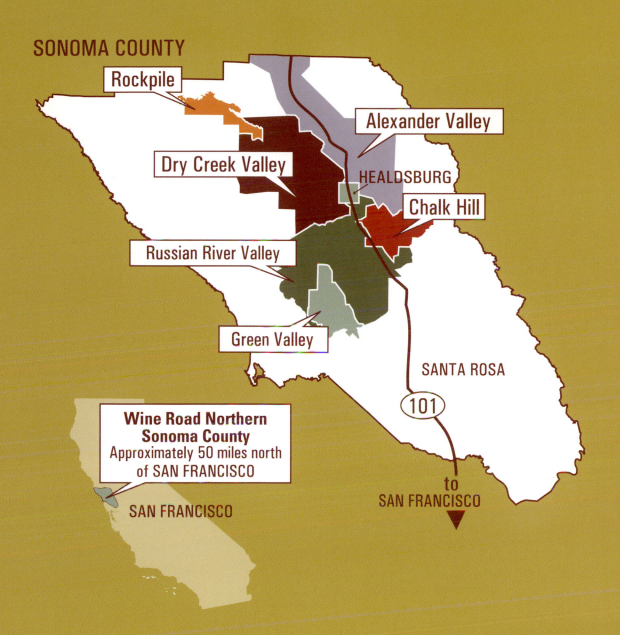

SONOMA COUNTY

Rockpile

Alexander Valley

Dry Creek Valley

HEALDSBURG

Chalk Hill

Russian River Valley

Green Valley

Wine Road Northern Sonoma County
Approximately 50 miles north of SAN FRANCISCO

SAN FRANCISCO

SANTA ROSA

101

to
SAN FRANCISCO

WINE ROAD NORTHERN SONOMA COUNTY

WINE ROAD GIVES BACK

In May 2011, Wine Road Executive Director Beth Costa and President Bruce Thomas of Mill Creek Winery presented the Redwood Empire Food Bank with a portion of the proceeds from this year's 33rd Annual Barrel Tasting. More than 140 wineries located in the Alexander, Dry Creek and Russian River valleys threw open their cellar doors for the 2011 event and during the two weekends, raised an impressive $30,000 for the Food Bank.

The Redwood Empire Food Bank serves 60,000 people in Sonoma, Mendocino, Lake, Humboldt and Del Norte counties each month, including children, seniors and working families.

"The Wine Road is proud to support the Redwood Empire Food Bank and in turn, those in need in the community," Costa says. "We are so proud of the fact that our contributions to this organization over the last five years now total more than $150,000. Our members can truly be proud."

This year's $30,000 donation was a combination of $26,000 from the Wine Road and $4,000 from customers who donated when ordering tickets.

$1 from every ticket sold from all Wine Road events and our "Ticket to the Wine Road" is donated to the Redwood Empire Food Bank. For more information about REFB or to make a donation, visit www.refb.com.

David Goodman of REFB, Beth Costa from Wine Road and Bruce Thomas from Mill Creek Winery

IT'S GOOD TO BE GREEN...

The winds of change are blowing along the Wine Road...

We're looking at our surroundings and finding ways that we can make sure our environmental impact is as minimal as possible.

Starting in 2008, the Wine Road began reducing plastic waste by providing event attendees with Calistoga drinking water from refillable, multi-gallon containers. Guests dispense water directly into their event wine glasses, instead of drinking from individual plastic bottles or using paper cups.

After the events, these water containers are returned to the Calistoga Beverage Co., to be refilled and used time and time again.

To reduce paper consumption, Wine Road no longer mails event invitations to the thousands of people on our mailing list. Instead, we reach out to our guests via online invitations. We count on everyone to help us spread the word about our events and happenings, and have added "share" buttons to our website so that you can easily e-mail all the news to friends and family.

In addition, we no longer print and mail tickets; guests simply order online and print e-tickets at home. Detailed event programs are available in PDF format on our website. Rather than mailing newsletters, we keep visitors updated via online sources; follow us on Facebook and Twitter. Sign up for our e-mail news, which we send out monthly, with lodging specials and event information from our members.

For details on these annual Wine Road events and other member winery events visit www.wineroad.com